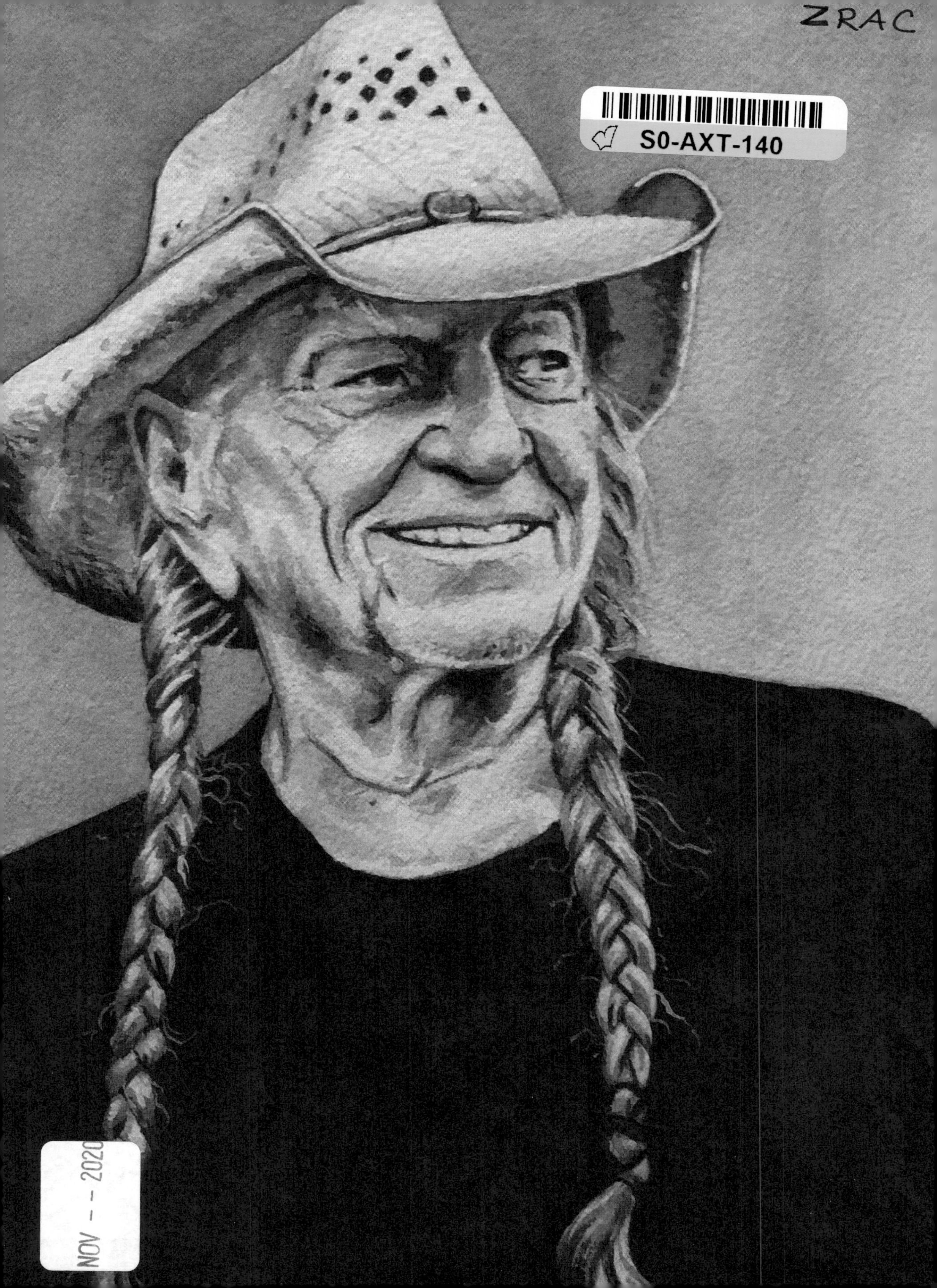

WILLIE NELSON

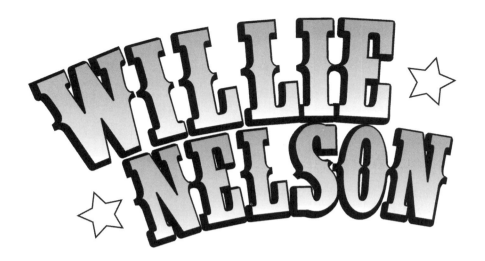

CONTENTS

INTRO, OUTRO, CHAPTER, AND ENDPAPER ILLUSTRATIONS BY ADAM WALMSLEY

ISBN 9781681122625

© 2020 T.J. Kirsch and each respective artist.
All rights reserved and managed by NBM Publishing, Inc.
Library of Congress Control Number: 2020940114
Printed in China
First printing September 2020
This book is also available wherever e-books are sold, ISBN 9781681122632

nbm
GRAPHIC NOVELS
Comics Biographies

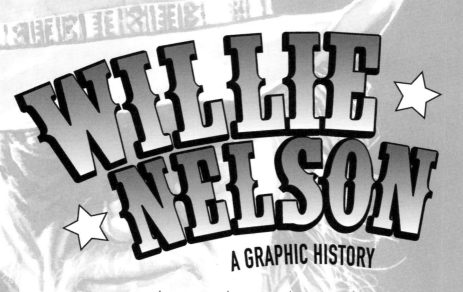

WILLIE NELSON

A GRAPHIC HISTORY

★ ★ ★ ★

WRITTEN BY T.J. KIRSCH
ILLUSTRATED BY: ADAM WALMSLEY, COŞKUN KUZGUN,
JEREMY MASSIE, HÅVARD S. JOHANSEN,
JESSE LONERGAN, JASON PITTMAN,
J.T. YOST, T.J. KIRSCH

nbm GRAPHIC NOVELS
Nantier · Beall · Minoustchine
NEW YORK

WILLIE HUGH NELSON.

FOR OVER 70 YEARS, HE'S BEEN PLAYING TO ADORING FANS, WRITTEN COUNTLESS SONGS AND ALBUMS, AND BECOME A WORLDWIDE COUNTRY MUSIC ICON.

THAT'S A HIGHLY UNLIKELY OUTCOME FOR ANY CHILD BORN IN THE MIDST OF A DEPRESSION IN SPARSELY POPULATED ABBOTT - LOCATED IN HILL COUNTY, TEXAS.

EVEN MORE UNLIKELY IS THE CONSTANT REINVENTION OF THE MAN, HIS GENRE-HOPPING CAREER(S), AND HIS FANDOM THAT SPANS SEVERAL GENERATIONS.

FROM HIS ABBOTT HIGH SCHOOL DAYS PLAYING BEER JOINTS AND SCHOOL DANCES...

...TO SELLING OUT LARGE VENUES, STILL, MORE THAN A HALF CENTURY LATER.

BUT HOW DID HE DO IT? HOW DID WILLIE BECOME AN ENDURING SUCCESS AND A HOUSEHOLD NAME?

CHAPTER 1

★ HILL COUNTY, TEXAS ★

WILLIE HUGH NELSON WAS BORN IN ABBOTT, TEXAS IN 1933.

Abbott
CITY LIMIT
POP. 356

TOO WILD, YOUNG, AND FREE SPIRITED TO PARENT, IRA AND MYRLE GIVE UP WILLIE, AND HE'S RAISED WITH LOVE BY HIS MATERNAL GRANDPARENTS.

AFFECTIONATELY CALLED MAMA AND DADDY NELSON, THEY ALSO RAISED WILLIE'S OLDER SISTER BOBBIE.

WHILE ATTENDING A NEARBY CHURCH REVIVAL PICNIC, YOUNG WILLIE RECITED A NOW-INFAMOUS POEM THAT SEEMED TO SET THE TONE FOR HIS LIFE.

WHAT ARE YOU LOOKING AT ME FOR? I AIN'T GOT NOTHIN' TO SAY.

IF YOU DON'T LIKE THE LOOKS OF ME, YOU CAN LOOK THE OTHER WAY!

HE'D BEEN PICKING HIS NOSE OUT OF NERVOUSNESS, AND BLOOD BEGINS RUNNING DOWN HIS FACE AND ONTO HIS BRIGHT WHITE SAILOR SUIT, WORD GETS OUT TO OTHER KIDS HIS AGE, AND HE EARNS THE NICKNAME 'BOOGER RED.'

YOUNG WILLIE SPENT MUCH OF HIS TIME READING COMIC BOOKS, WRITING POETRY AND WRITING SONGS.

HE CAME ACROSS ADS FOR A SELF DEFENSE COURSE IN AN EARLY SUPERHERO COMIC – A PRACTICE WHICH WILLIE WOULD ALSO CONTINUE AS AN ADULT.

BUT HIS MOST NOTABLE CHILDHOOD PASSION WAS – OF COURSE – MUSIC.

SUMMER DAYS WERE SOMETIMES FILLED WITH WORK IN THE COTTON FIELDS IN ABBOTT, BUT AT NIGHT WILLIE, HIS FRIEND ZEKE AND OTHERS WOULD FIND PLENTY OF WAYS TO HAVE FUN.

SOME ACTIVITIES WERE MORE DANGEROUS THAN OTHERS.

WILLIE HUGH! WHAT IN GOD'S NAME HAVE YOU BEEN DOING? MY POOR BOY!

BATTLE WOUNDS, MAMA!

EVEN WITH ALL THE HIJINX AND TROUBLEMAKING, THE MUSIC WAS WILLIE'S CONSTANT.

FOR THAT MOONLIT PASS BY THE ALAMO AND ROSE, MY ROSE OF SAN ANTOOOONNE...

AND SOON, HE DISCOVERED HE COULD ALSO USE HIS MUSICAL TALENT AND SKILL TO EARN MONEY.

ALTHOUGH AT FIRST IT DIDN'T SEEM QUITE LUCRATIVE ENOUGH FOR THE YOUNG MUSICIAN.

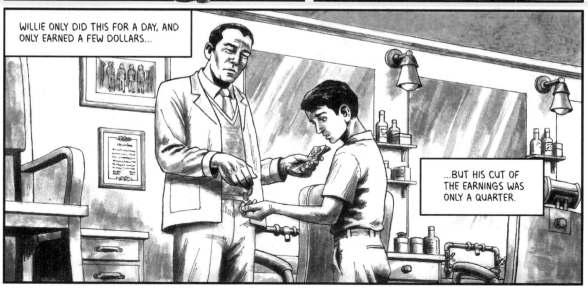

WILLIE ONLY DID THIS FOR A DAY, AND ONLY EARNED A FEW DOLLARS...

...BUT HIS CUT OF THE EARNINGS WAS ONLY A QUARTER.

WILLIE SHOWED AN INTEREST IN PLAYING LIVE MUSIC FAIRLY EARLY - FROM SCHOOL DANCES TO PLAYING LOCAL BEER JOINTS WITH JOHN REJCEK'S FIFTEEN PERSON POLKA BAND.

MAMA NELSON WASN'T THRILLED ABOUT YOUNG WILLIE PLAYING MUSIC IN BARS, BUT AFTER MONEY WAS BROUGHT UP...

IN THE SUMMERS, I WORK IN THE FIELDS ALL WEEK FOR EIGHT DOLLARS.

THAT'S WHAT MR. REJCEK PAID ME FOR ONLY ONE NIGHT IN WACO.

SHE SEEMED TO CHANGE HER TUNE.

FROM THAT POINT ON, THERE WAS NEVER A COMPLAINT FROM MAMA NELSON.

WILLIE'S SISTER BOBBIE MARRIED WHILE STILL ATTENDING ABBOTT HIGH SCHOOL, AND HER HUSBAND BUD FLETCHER HELMED THEIR NEW BAND, BUD FLETCHER AND THE TEXANS.

WE SHOULD START A **COMBO.**

SISTER BOBBIE PLAYED PIANO, WILLIE SANG AND PLAYED GUITAR, AND BUD STUCK A BROOM HANDLE INTO A BUCKET OF SAND AND WHACKED IT LIKE A BASS.

MAMA NELSON WASN'T THRILLED ABOUT THE MARRIAGE, BUT WELCOMED THE EXTRA INCOME.

WILLIE WAS PLAYING CONSISTENTLY, MAKING A LITTLE MONEY, AND GAINING FANS, ONE AT A TIME.

THE BAND EVEN SECURED THEIR OWN REGULAR SHOW ON **KBHR** IN HILLSBORO, TEXAS.

ANOTHER FORMATIVE LEARNING EXPERIENCE FOR WILLIE WAS PUTTING TOGETHER A LIVE LOCAL SHOW AND INVITING BOB WILLS AND HIS TEXAS PLAYBOYS TO PLAY AT A VENUE IN NEARBY LAKE WHITNEY.

THIS WAS AN AMBITIOUS PLAN FOR THE TEENAGE WILLIE TO TAKE ON, BUT HE HAD TO TRY. EVEN IF THE SHOW MADE NO MONEY, HE'D STILL HAVE HIMSELF A FRONT ROW SEAT TO SEE ONE OF HIS HEROES.

YES, THAT'S RIGHT FOLKS, **BOB WILLS**, KING OF WESTERN SWING WILL BE APPEARING WITH HIS TEXAS PLAYBOYS IN **LAKE WHITNEY**! COME AND SEE THE KING! TICKETS AVAILABLE AT THE GATE!

ON THE NIGHT OF THE SHOW, WILLIE OBSERVED HOW BOB COULD READ THE AUDIENCE, ADJUST ACCORDINGLY, AND HOLD THEIR ATTENTION FOR HOURS.

IT WAS QUITE THE LEARNING EXPERIENCE, DESPITE HAVING TO HAND OVER MOST OF THE EARNINGS FROM TICKET SALES FOR BOB WILLS' FEE.

YOU'RE **ALRIGHT, KID.** I'LL SEE YOU 'ROUND.

AS THE TOUR BUS PULLED AWAY, WILLIE FELT A GREAT SENSE OF ACCOMPLISHMENT – EVERYONE WHO ATTENDED ENJOYED THE SHOW.

DURING HIGH SCHOOL, WHEN HE WASN'T PLAYING MUSIC, WILLIE WAS ALSO BUSY WITH SEVERAL SPORTS, INCLUDING FOOTBALL AND BASKETBALL.

BUT AFTER GRADUATING, HE WONDERED WHAT WAS NEXT.

AND AFTER A VERY SHORT STINT AS A TREE TRIMMER — IN WHICH HE ALMOST LOST A FINGER...

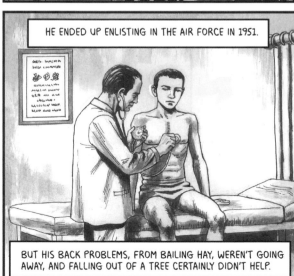

HE ENDED UP ENLISTING IN THE AIR FORCE IN 1951.

BUT HIS BACK PROBLEMS, FROM BAILING HAY, WEREN'T GOING AWAY, AND FALLING OUT OF A TREE CERTAINLY DIDN'T HELP.

WELL, LET'S SEE IF YOU CAN GET THROUGH BASIC TRAINING.

DESPITE HIS BACK INJURY, WILLIE EXCELLED IN HIS NEW MILITARY CAREER.

BUT AFTER A WHILE, THAT CAREER WASN'T QUITE PANNING OUT. HE WAS SHUFFLED TO SEVERAL OTHER BASES AND JOBS, AND EVENTUALLY RE-INJURED HIS BACK DOING GRUNT WORK.

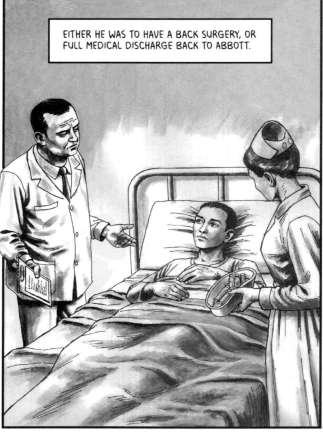

EITHER HE WAS TO HAVE A BACK SURGERY, OR FULL MEDICAL DISCHARGE BACK TO ABBOTT.

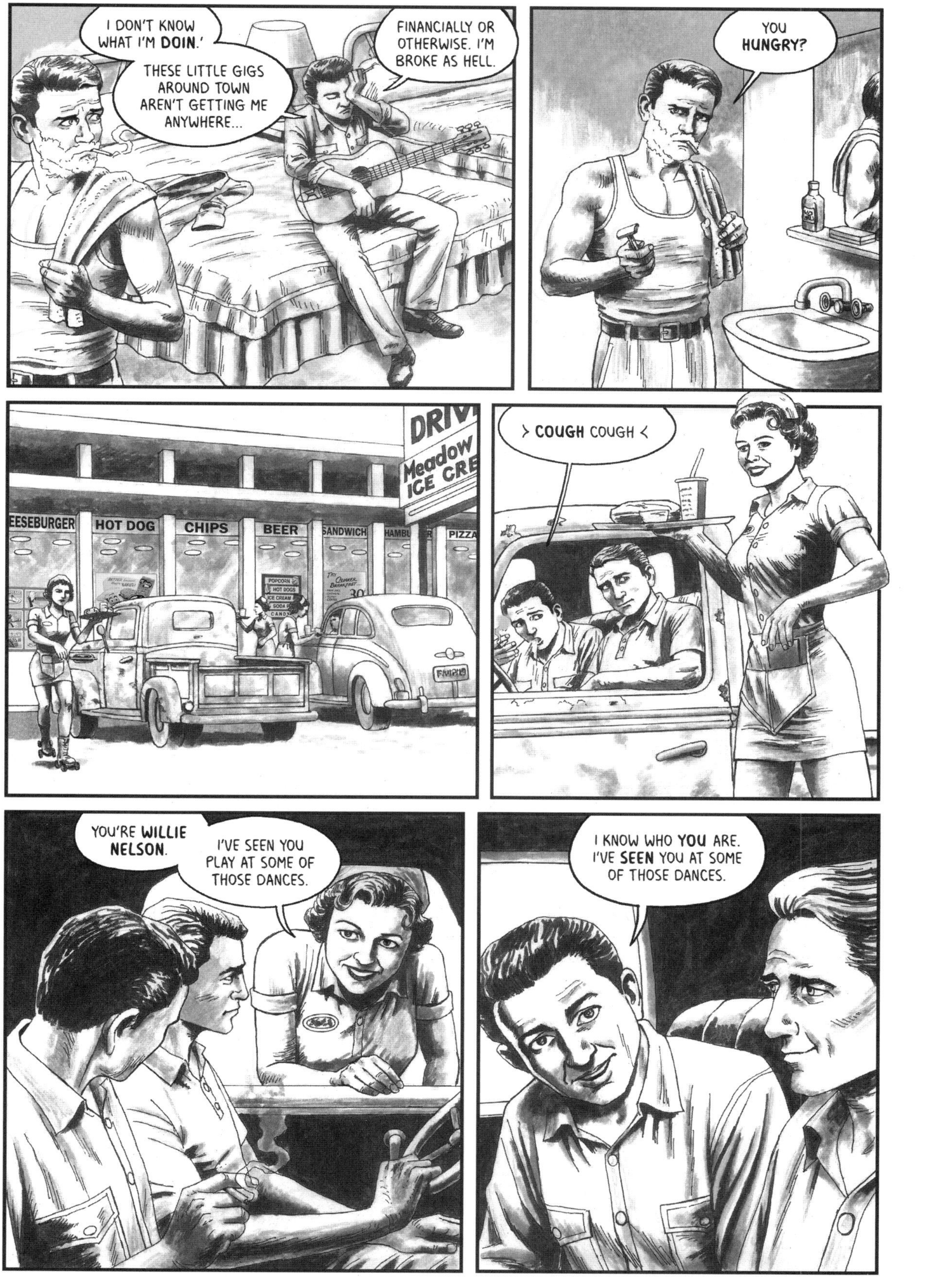

I DON'T KNOW WHAT I'M DOIN.'
THESE LITTLE GIGS AROUND TOWN AREN'T GETTING ME ANYWHERE...
FINANCIALLY OR OTHERWISE. I'M BROKE AS HELL.
YOU HUNGRY?
DRIV
Meadow ICE CRE
EESEBURGER
HOT DOG
CHIPS
BEER
SANDWICH
PIZZA
POPCORN
HOT DOGS
ICE CREAM
> COUGH COUGH <
YOU'RE WILLIE NELSON.
I'VE SEEN YOU PLAY AT SOME OF THOSE DANCES.
I KNOW WHO YOU ARE. I'VE SEEN YOU AT SOME OF THOSE DANCES.

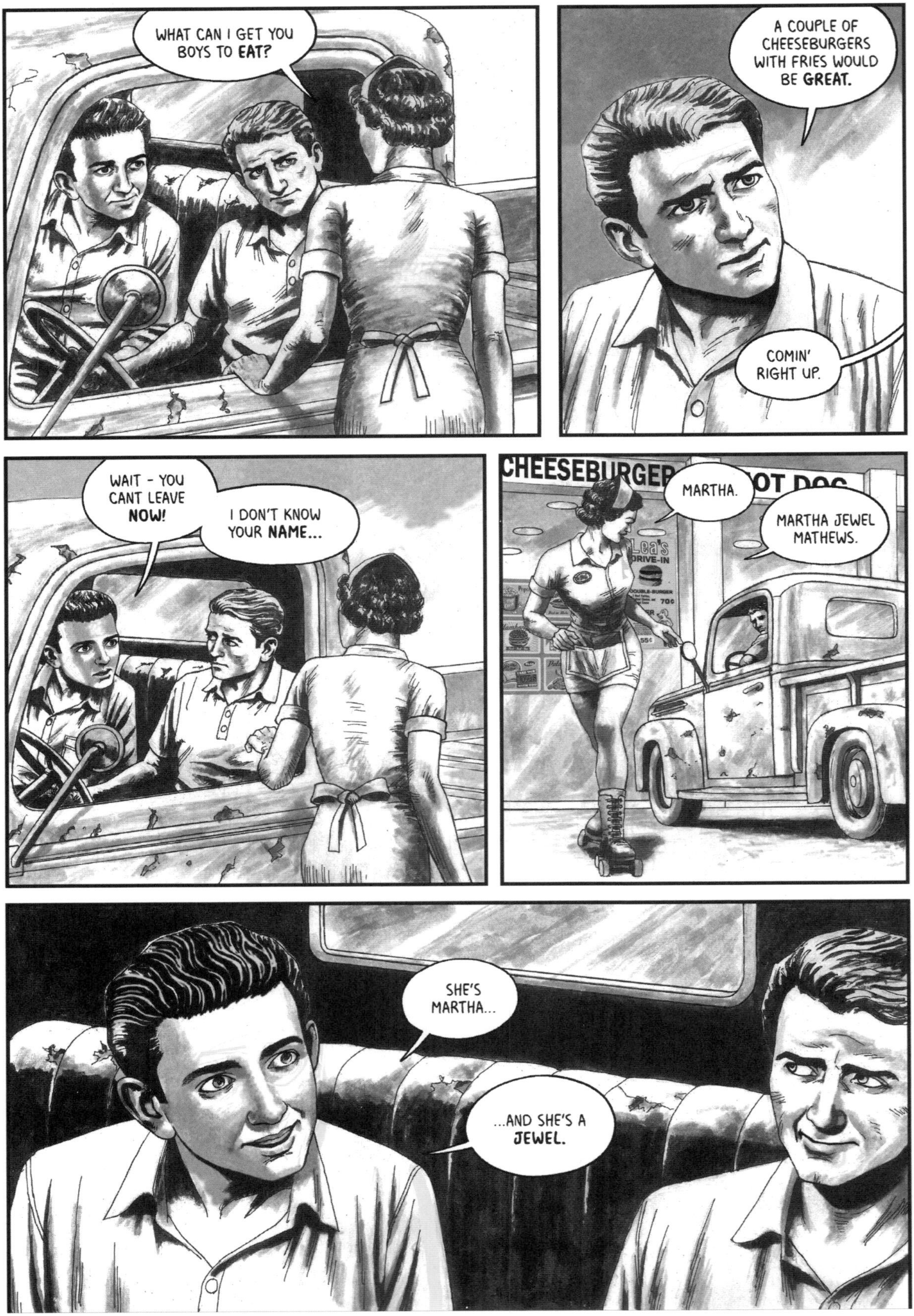
WHAT CAN I GET YOU BOYS TO EAT?
A COUPLE OF CHEESEBURGERS WITH FRIES WOULD BE GREAT.
COMIN' RIGHT UP.
WAIT - YOU CANT LEAVE NOW!
I DON'T KNOW YOUR NAME...
CHEESEBURGER
OT DOG
MARTHA.
MARTHA JEWEL MATHEWS.
Lea's DRIVE-IN
DOUBLE-BURGER
70¢
55¢
SHE'S MARTHA...
...AND SHE'S A JEWEL.

CHAPTER 2

★ A HUMBLE PICKER ★

WASTING NO TIME, WILLIE AND MARTHA WENT AND GOT MARRIED. SHE HAD A LETTER TO SHOW THE JUSTICE OF THE PEACE, SAYING SHE WAS OF LEGAL AGE, EVEN THOUGH SHE WAS SIXTEEN.

WILLIE, YOU'RE GOING TO HAVE TO GET A JOB AND HELP WITH BILLS IF THIS IS GOING TO WORK.

YOU'RE BOTH GOING TO HAVE TO WORK.

MAMA NELSON WASN'T TOO HAPPY, BUT SHE ALLOWED THEM TO LIVE IN THE HOUSE FOR THE TIME BEING.

IN ADDITION TO HIS MUSICAL PURSUITS, WILLIE SUPPLEMENTED HIS INCOME AT THE TIME BY WORKING AT A SADDLE FACTORY.

TOO SCARED OF INJURING HIS HANDS, WHICH WOULDN'T BE IDEAL FOR A MUSICIAN... HE QUIT FAIRLY EARLY INTO THE JOB.

MARTHA, HOWEVER, COULD ALWAYS FIND WAITRESSING WORK.

COFFEE 5¢

THE NEW MARRIED COUPLE HAD AN INTENSE, TUMULTUOUS RELATIONSHIP, AND THERE WAS ALSO JEALOUSY ALMOST INSTANTLY.

I'VE BEEN WATCHIN' YOU MAKE EYES AT THAT LITTLE WHORE ALL NIGHT, WILLIE NELSON!!

A CHANGE OF SCENERY WAS SOMETHING THEY BOTH AGREED WAS NEEDED AFTER MONTHS OF FIGHTING.

SO THEY PACKED UP EVERYTHING THEY HAD INTO A BORROWED CAR, AND HEADED TO WILLIE'S MOTHER'S PLACE IN EUGENE, OREGON.

AND ONCE AGAIN, IN EUGENE, MARTHA QUICKLY FOUND WORK AS A WAITRESS...

...AND WILLIE FOUND SOME WORK IN A BAND.

WHEN MARTHA CAME HOME, WILLIE OFTEN SUSPECTED HER ABUNDANCE OF TIPS WAS A RESULT OF FLIRTING WITH CUSTOMERS.

THIS LEVEL OF SUSPICION BETWEEN THE TWO WAS CONSTANT...

...AND BOTH WILLIE AND MARTHA AGREED IT WAS TIME TO MOVE BACK TO TEXAS. SPECIFICALLY WACO. WILLIE THOUGHT MAYBE HE COULD MAKE A NAME FOR HIMSELF CLOSER TO HOME.

AFTER SETTLING IN, WILLIE DECIDED TO ENROLL AS A STUDENT AT BAYLOR UNIVERSITY FOR A FEW MONTHS, UNTIL HIS G.I. BILL MONEY RAN OUT.

IT DIDN'T WORK OUT, ESPECIALLY SINCE WILLIE "MAJORED IN DOMINOES."

ONE THING THAT MARTHA AND WILLIE HAD WAS A LOVE OF FAMILY.

AND THAT'S WHY THEY WERE BOTH SO ELATED WHEN THEY FOUND OUT MARTHA WAS PREGNANT WITH THEIR FIRST CHILD LANA IN 1953.

BUT THE EXCITEMENT OVER THE NEWS WAS SHORT LIVED, AS WILLIE'S PROFESSIONAL STRUGGLES CONTINUED.

HE WASN'T FINDING ENOUGH GIGS, AND BEGAN SELLING ENCYCLOPEDIAS DOOR TO DOOR.

WILLIE WAS A DAMN GOOD SALESMAN, AND COULD TURN ON THE CHARM...

BUT ALWAYS FELT GUILTY AFTERWARDS. NO FAMILY WHO IS STRUGGLING SHOULD BE SPENDING HARD-EARNED SAVINGS ON A BRAND NEW SET OF EXPENSIVE REFERENCE BOOKS.

AS THE OPPORTUNITIES IN WACO DECLINED, THEY DECIDED TO TRY YET ANOTHER, BIGGER CITY - SAN ANTONIO.

AND SHORTLY AFTER THE MOVE, WILLIE AND MARTHA WELCOMED LANA, THEIR FIRST BORN.

AND THAT DAY, THE WORLD CHANGED FOR WILLIE. HE WANTED TO BE THERE FOR HER, AS HIS GRANDFATHER WAS FOR HIM

A STRONG AND STEADY POSITIVE INFLUENCE.

SOON, HOWEVER, THINGS WENT DOWNHILL IN THE NELSON HOUSEHOLD.

ONE NIGHT, AFTER WILLIE CAME HOME DRUNK, HE PASSED OUT ON THE BED NEXT TO MARTHA.

SHE'D FINALLY HAD ENOUGH.

SHE WAS SO UPSET AND FRUSTRATED, THAT SHE TIED HIM UP IN A PILLOWCASE...

AND BEAT HIM WITH A BROOM.

PUTTING ASIDE THE DRAMA OF HIS HOMELIFE, WILLIE HIT THE DIVERSE NIGHTCLUB CIRCUIT IN SAN ANTONIO WITH ENTHUSIASM.

THERE WERE FIVE MILITARY BASES IN THE CITY, ENSURING THERE'D ALWAYS BE PEOPLE LOOKING FOR A GOOD TIME.

HE QUICKLY MET MANY MUSICIANS, LIKE JOHNNY BUSH – AND DECIDED TO FORM A BAND WITH HIM CALLED THE MISSION CITY PLAYBOYS.

UNFORTUNATELY THE GROUP FIZZLED OUT FASTER THAN IT WAS FORMED.

WHILE STILL PLAYING NIGHTCLUBS FURIOUSLY AROUND SAN ANTONIO, WILLIE COULD STILL BARELY MAKE ANY KIND OF LIVING WAGE.

SO HE QUICKLY ANSWERED AN AD FOR AN ON-AIR DJ AT A NEARBY RADIO STATION IN PLEASANTON.

DR. BEN PARKER HANDED WILLIE SOME ON-AIR COPY TO READ LIVE ON THE AIR AS AN IMPROMPTU AUDITION.

THE PLEASANTON PHARMACY'S PHARMACEUTICAL DEPARTMENT ACCURATELY AND PRECISELY FILLS YOUR DOCTOR'S PRESCRIPTIONS.

EXCELLENT, YOUNG MAN. YOU HAVE A JOB.

WILLIE ALSO TOOK ADVANTAGE OF THE RECORDING EQUIPMENT AT KBOP TO, FOR THE FIRST TIME, CUT A RECORD WITH A FEW ORIGINAL SONGS.

HE SENT COPIES TO A SMALL RECORD LABEL IN TEXAS, BUT NEVER HEARD BACK.

EVEN THOUGH THERE WERE CONSTANT SETBACKS, WILLIE KEPT ON PURSUING HIS SINGING AND SONGWRITING.

AND WITH THAT CAME THE CONSTANT TEMPTATIONS OF WILLING WOMEN.

SOON, THE TENSIONS BETWEEN WILLIE AND MARTHA WERE AT AN ALL-TIME HIGH, AND THEY AGAIN PACKED UP AND MOVED TO FORT WORTH FOR A FRESH START, AND TO BE CLOSE TO SISTER BOBBIE.

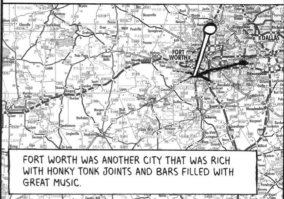

FORT WORTH WAS ANOTHER CITY THAT WAS RICH WITH HONKY TONK JOINTS AND BARS FILLED WITH GREAT MUSIC.

HE SOON FOUND A JOB AS A DISC JOCKEY IN FORT WORTH, KCNC, WHERE HE CAME UP WITH HIS NEW ON-AIR CATCHPHRASE FOR HIS SHOW 'WESTERN EXPRESS.'

ON AIR

THIS IS YOUR OLD COTTON-PICKIN', SNUFF-DIPPIN', TOBACCA-CHEWIN', STUMP-JUMPIN', GRAVY-SOPPIN', COFFEE POT-DODGIN', DUMPLIN EATIN', FROG-GIGGIN' HILLBILLY FROM **HILL COUNTY, TEXAS!**

HE'D OPEN EVERY SHOW WITH 'RED HEADED STRANGER' BY GUITAR BOOGIE SMITH...

...AND EVERY TIME, WILLIE WOULD DEDICATE THE SONG TO HIS BABY DAUGHTER LANA.

THIS ONE'S FOR **MY LITTLE GIRL.**

WHEN HE GOT HOME AT NIGHT, LANA ALWAYS WANTED WILLIE TO SING THE SONG TO HER UNTIL SHE FELL ASLEEP.

IT WAS AROUND THIS TIME IN FORT WORTH WHEN FRED LOCKWOOD, A LOCAL MUSICIAN, INTRODUCED WILLIE TO SMOKING MARIJUANA.

WE'D PROBABLY GET HAPPIER FASTER IF WE BLEW SOME TEA.

NEVER TRIED IT.

A MEMBER OF THE COMMUNIST PARTY...

BUT HE WAS WORRIED, LIKE A LOT OF PEOPLE IN MIDDLE AMERICA WHO'D SEEN 'REEFER MADNESS' – THAT POT WOULD DRIVE HIM INSANE.

NO, YOU DUMB SON OF A BITCH!

YOU DON'T TREAT IT LIKE NO LUCKY STRIKE – YOU HOLD IN THE FUCKIN' SMOKE! WATCH.

WILLIE TRIED AGAIN, AND FOR THE FIRST TIME, GOT HIGH.

FOR YEARS TO COME, BOOZE WOULD STILL BE WILLIE'S VICE OF CHOICE – NOT YET BEING UP TO SPEED ON ALL THE MEDICAL BENEFITS OF MARIJUANA.

MR. MCCARTHY!!! PLEASE...

IN KEEPING WITH HIS SOMETIMES WILDLY CONTRADICTORY WAY OF LIVING, WILLIE ALSO TAUGHT SUNDAY SCHOOL TO KIDS AT THE LOCAL BAPTIST CHURCH.

AND HE WAS ALSO BAPTIZED THERE AS WELL, AS AN ADULT.

THIS DEEPENED WILLIE'S FAITH A GREAT DEAL.

AND FOR A MOMENT, IN BETWEEN THE CHAOS AND UNCERTAINTIES OF WILLIE'S CURRENT LIFE...

THERE WAS SOME PEACE.

THE NELSON FAMILY'S PATTERN OF WANDERLUST SOON CONTINUED. AS EXCITED AND MOTIVATED AS WILLIE AND MARTHA WERE TO START OVER YET AGAIN, IN SUNNY SAN DIEGO...THINGS DIDN'T PAN OUT NEARLY AS WELL AS THEY'D HOPED.

MARTHA, YET AGAIN, FOUND WAITRESSING WORK TO SUPPORT THE FAMILY, BUT WILLIE WAS UNABLE TO FIND ANY WORK AT ALL. NOT RADIO WORK. NOTHING.

AND NO ONE WOULD HIRE HIM AS A SIDEMAN OR PICKER, OR SINGER, IF HE WASN'T IN CALIFORNIA'S UNION.

WILLIE WAS DEPRESSED, HOPELESS AND WITHOUT ANY PROSPECTS...SO HE DECIDED TO CUT OUT IN THE MIDDLE OF THE NIGHT, AND HEAD NORTH TO HIS MOTHER MYRLE'S.

CHAPTER 3

★ COUNTRY WILLIE ★

AFTER A DIFFICULT JOURNEY, WILLIE FINALLY MADE IT TO HIS MOTHER MYRLE'S HOUSE IN THE MIDDLE OF THE NIGHT IN PORTLAND, OREGON.

MARTHA, PREGNANT WITH SUSIE, ALSO ARRIVED WITH LANA SOON AFTER. ALL SEEMED FORGIVEN.

WILLIE FOUND WORK AS A PLUMBER'S HELPER - JUST TO HAVE SOME MONEY COMING IN - WHILE SETTLING INTO THE MUSIC SCENE.

MARTHA FOUND A WAITRESS JOB QUICKLY IN PORTLAND...

...WHILE WILLIE SOON FOUND OUT ABOUT A JOB OPENING AT VANCOUVER, WASHINGTON'S WELL-KNOWN KVAN RADIO STATION - RIGHT ACROSS THE RIVER FROM PORTLAND.

WILLIE GOT THE GIG, AND THE STATION HEAVILY PROMOTED HIS 'WESTERN EXPRESS' SHOW IN LOTS OF NEWSPAPER ADS AND IN-STORE APPEARANCES - WITH WILLIE TOUTING A DAVY CROCKETT-ESQUE OUTFIT.

WHILE WILLIE WAS BUILDING A NAME FOR HIMSELF AT KVAN AND IN THE LOCAL MUSIC SCENE, HIS SECOND DAUGHTER SUSIE ARRIVED IN EARLY 1957.

MARTHA'S MOTHER AND FATHER MOVED NEARBY TO HELP TAKE CARE OF THE GIRLS, AND WILLIE AND MARTHA FOUND A SMALL MEXICAN ADOBE-STYLE HOUSE WITH A BARN FOR THEM TO SETTLE INTO.

WHILE WORKING AT KVAN, NOT ONLY WAS WILLIE SPINNING POPULAR SONGS LIKE JOHNNY CASH'S 'THERE YOU GO' AND ELVIS PRESLEY'S HEARTBREAK HOTEL...'

BUT HE USED THE RECORDING EQUIPMENT TO CUT HIS OWN RECORD, 'NO PLACE FOR ME,' WITH A B-SIDE OF 'LUMBERJACK,' A SONG BY HIS FRIEND LEON PAYNE.

WILLIE WAS ALSO IN A UNIQUE POSITION TO PEDDLE THAT RECORD ON-AIR, USING HIS OWN RADIO SHOW. WITH THAT ADDED PROMOTION, HE SOLD A FEW THOUSAND COPIES BY MAIL ORDER.

FOR THE LOW, LOW PRICE OF **ONE MEASLY DOLLAR**, I'LL SEND YOU A COPY OF **TEXAS WILLIE NELSON'S LATEST RELEASE** - THE SONG 'NO PLACE FOR ME.'

ALONG WITH A SIGNED GLOSSY PHOTO OF WILLIE HIMSELF.

HE WAS PROVIDING FOR HIS FAMILY, FINALLY. CONTENT, AT TIMES - BUT WILLIE WAS STILL QUITE UNSATISFIED WITH HIS CURRENT CAREER'S PROGRESS.

WHILE WORKING AT KVAN, WILLIE ENCOUNTERED NOTED SONGWRITER MAE BOREN AXTON ('HEARTBREAK HOTEL', AMONG OTHERS), WHO CAME THROUGH TOWN TO PROMOTE A HANK SNOW RECORD ON 'WESTERN EXPRESS.'

WILLIE? MAE AXTON'S WALKING THROUGH.

BEFORE LEAVING THE STATION, MS. AXTON WAS STOPPED BY WILLIE. HE INTRODUCED HIMSELF AND ASKED IF SHE HAD TIME TO LISTEN TO A SONG.

I'VE GOT A PLANE TO CATCH, SON.

I'D BE MUCH OBLIGED.

WILLIE HAD A TREMENDOUS AMOUNT OF RESPECT FOR MS. AXTON AND HER WORK.

SHE RELUCTANTLY AGREED. WILLIE PLAYED A FEW OF HIS ORIGINALS ON GUITAR, AND AFTERWARDS HE HAD HER LISTEN TO A DEMO HE JUST RECORDED, ON A SMALL JAPANESE REEL-TO-REEL, CALLED 'FAMILY BIBLE.'

OKAY THEN, SON. I'LL TAKE THE TIME.

There's a family bible on the table
each page is torn and hard to read
but the family bible on the table
will ever be my key to memories
at the end of day when work was over
and when the evening meal was done
dad would read to us from the family bible
and we'd count our many blessings,
one by one...

IT WAS CLEAR THAT MS. AXTON HEARD THE TALENT IN WILLIE'S WRITING.

SON, YOU HAVE SOMETHING.

I DO?

YOU HAVE A PRECIOUS GIFT.

I WISH I HAD MORE TIME TO SPEND WITH YOU, BECAUSE THERE'S MORE I CAN TELL YOU.

FOR NOW, JUST REMEMBER TWO THINGS. THE FIRST IS THAT YOU'RE LOOKING AT A LADY WHO, IF SHE HAD HALF OF YOUR WRITING TALENT, WOULD BE THE HAPPIEST GAL ON EARTH

AND SECONDLY, IF YOU'RE TO DEVELOP THAT TALENT, YOU CAN'T KEEP HIDING OUT HERE IN THE NORTHWEST.

YOU'VE GOT TO MOVE ON, SON. QUIT THIS JOB, AND YOU GO TO TEXAS OR TENNESSEE AND YOU **WRITE.**

I DON'T HAVE A LOT OF MONEY, BUT I CAN ALWAYS RAISE A COUPLE HUNDRED DOLLARS.

WILLIE COULDN'T HELP BUT FOLLOW THE ADVICE HE'D GOTTEN THAT DAY AT KVAN. ALTHOUGH IT WASN'T IMMEDIATE, HE DID EVENTUALLY GET BACK TO TEXAS.

PRIOR TO THE MOVE TO TEXAS, THOUGH, WILLIE AND FAMILY STOPPED IN DENVER, COLORADO FIRST. WILLIE WORKED AS A PICKER IN A HONKY TONK CALLED HEART'S CORNER FOR A FEW WEEKS.

THEN THE NELSONS WENT ONTO SPRINGFIELD, MISSOURI, WHERE WILLIE HAD A FRIEND IN MUSICIAN BILLY WALKER.

WILLIE WORKED AS A DISHWASHER BRIEFLY, AFTER AN AUDITION BILLY WALKER SET UP DIDN'T QUITE WORK OUT. MARTHA WAITED TABLES WHILE THE FAMILY STRUGGLED TO MAKE ENDS MEET.

MARTHA LUCKILY KNEW BILLY WALKER'S WIFE. THEY WERE OLD FRIENDS FROM TEXAS, AND THIS MUST HAVE PROVIDED SOME STABILITY WHILE THEY WERE MOVING SO OFTEN.

SOON WILLIE AND FAMILY ENDED UP BACK IN TEXAS – IN FORT WORTH. THEY INITIALLY STAYED WITH WILLIE'S FATHER AND HIS WIFE LORRAINE. BY THIS POINT, MARTHA WAS PREGNANT WITH THEIR THIRD CHILD, WILLIE HUGH NELSON JR, LATER KNOWN AS BILLY.

WILLIE STRUGGLED TO MAKE A DECENT LIVING PLAYING MUSIC. IN FORT WORTH, HE FIRST GOT A JOB PUMPING GAS AND CHANGING OIL AT A GAS STATION. IT WAS OWNED BY PAUL TRACY, SECOND HUSBAND OF WILLIE'S SISTER BOBBIE.

BUT TO WILLIE, THE WAGES WEREN'T ENOUGH. HE WENT BACK TO SELLING ENCYCLOPEDIAS DOOR TO DOOR, WHERE THE INCOME POTENTIAL WAS MUCH GREATER. THIS TIME, HE WORKED FOR ENCYCLOPEDIA AMERICANA.

AND WITH HIS FAMOUS WILLIE NELSON CHARM, HE MADE THREE SALES THE FIRST NIGHT. THE COMPANY LOVED HIM, OF COURSE, AND THEY EVEN WANTED TO PROMOTE HIM.

BUT THE ACT OF CONVINCING PEOPLE TO BUY SOMETHING THEY SOMETIMES COULDN'T AFFORD WEIGHED ON WILLIE. HE QUIT SOON AFTER, AND WENT FULL BORE BACK INTO THE HONKY TONK SCENE.

BUT EVEN LIVE MUSIC GIGS WEREN'T ALWAYS SMOOTH SAILING FOR WILLIE. HE'D SOMETIMES GET FIRED BECAUSE HIS PHRASING AND TIMING WERE SO UNUSUAL. THE MUSICIANS IN THE BAND HAD A DIFFICULT TIME FOLLOWING HIM, AND SOMETIMES PEOPLE HAD A HARD TIME DANCING TO THE MUSIC.

THE FAMILY SOON HIT THE ROAD AGAIN - FIRST BRIEFLY IN WACO, THEN SETTLED DOWN IN HOUSTON. STILL FUELED BY THE WORDS OF THE WISE MAE AXTON, WILLIE CONTINUED ON FULL STEAM AHEAD, DETERMINED TO MAKE A NAME FOR HIMSELF IN MUSIC

BY THE TIME WILLIE ARRIVED IN HOUSTON, HE ALREADY HAD A HANDFUL OF MEMORABLE, EVEN UNFORGETTABLE SONGS - ALTHOUGH NO ONE BUT WILLIE HIMSELF TOOK MUCH NOTICE.

WILLIE TOOK HIS SONGS 'MR. RECORD MAN,' 'NIGHT LIFE,' 'CRAZY,' AND 'FUNNY HOW TIME SLIPS AWAY,' AND PLAYED THEM FOR HIS FRIEND LARRY BUTLER. BUTLER HAD A BAND THAT PLAYED REGULARLY AT A PLACE CALLED THE ESQUIRE CLUB, ALONG THE HEMPSTEAD HIGHWAY.

WILLIE PITCHED THE SONGS TO LARRY TO PURCHASE THE RIGHTS, FOR TEN DOLLARS APIECE, BUT LARRY REFUSED.

YOU CAN'T SELL THESE SONGS, WILLIE. THEY'RE TOO GOOD. YOU NEED TO HOLD ONTO THEM YOURSELF. IF YOU NEED THE MONEY, I CAN LOAN YOU SOME.

WILLIE ENDED UP TAKING UP THE OFFER FOR A LOAN, AND WITH THAT MONEY, THE NELSON FAMILY PAID FOR AN APARTMENT IN PASADENA, JUST OUTSIDE OF HOUSTON.

"AND YOU CAN PAY ME BACK BY JOINING MY BAND AND WORKING AT THE CLUB HERE."

HE ALSO SCORED A GIG AT KCRT 650 AM IN PASADENA, WHICH HE USED TO HEAVILY PROMOTE HIS UPCOMING SHOWS.

SEE Y'ALL AT 8PM AT THE ESQUIRE BALLROOM. BE THERE! ME AND THE REST OF LARRY BUTLER'S SUNSET PLAYBOYS WILL BE THERE TOO, PLAYING OUR HEARTS OUT JUST FOR YOU.

EVEN WITH ALL OF WILLIE'S VARIOUS SOURCES OF INCOME, HE STILL ENDED UP BROKE PRETTY OFTEN. THIS LED HIM TO PITCH ANOTHER SONG, 'FAMILY BIBLE,' TO HIS FRIEND PAUL BUSKIRK, WHO OWNED A RECORDING STUDIO AND MUSIC SCHOOL.

WILLIE WAS STARTING TO HIT HIS STRIDE AS A SONGWRITER. WHEN PAUL BUKIRK HEARD THE SONG, HE DECIDED TO GO IN WITH TWO OTHER PEOPLE, AND BUY THE SONG - FOR A PRETTY MODEST AMOUNT OF $50.

IT WASN'T MUCH, BUT IT WAS SOMETHING. PAUL ALSO HIRED WILLIE TO TEACH GUITAR AT HIS MUSIC SCHOOL.

HOUSTON SEEMED TO BE A PLACE WHERE WILLIE'S CREATIVITY COULD BLOSSOM. DURING LONG DRIVES TO GIGS AND HIS VARIOUS JOBS, WILLIE WAS INSPIRED BY THE LANDSCAPES AND GRITTY CITYSCAPE OF THE AREA.

WHEREVER THE SONGS CAME FROM, THEY SURE FLOWED EASY DURING THOSE COMMUTES.

AND IF HE REMEMBERED THE LYRICS AND MELODY BY THE TIME HE GOT TO HIS DESTINATION, HE KNEW IT WAS GOOD. SOMETIMES HE'D RECORD THEM ON A SMALL REEL-TO-REEL TAPE RECORDER.

When the evenin' sun goes down
You will find me hangin' 'round
The night life ain't no good life
But it's my life

Many people just like me
Dreamin' of old used-to-be's
And the night life ain't no good life
But it's my life

AND THE SONGS CONTINUED TO FLOW...

I'm crazy, crazy for feeling so lonely
I'm crazy, crazy for feeling so blue

I knew, that you'd love me as long as you wanted
And then someday, you'd leave me for somebody new

Worry, why do I let myself worry?
Wondering, what in the world did I do?

THE LYRICS SEEMED TO COME OUT OF THIN AIR. THE STORIES CAME FROM HIS OWN LIFE. PEOPLE HE KNEW. HIS UNIQUE EXPERIENCES AND RELATIONSHIPS.

Well, hello there
My it's been a long, long time
How am I doin'?
Oh, I guess that I'm doin' fine
It's been so long now but it seems now
That it was only yesterday
Gee, ain't it funny how time slips away

RIDING HIGH ON THE SUCCESS AND PRIDE OF STARTING TO SELL SONGS HE WAS TRULY PROUD OF, WILLIE DECIDED IT WAS FINALLY TIME TO MOVE TO TO NASHVILLE.

FIRED FROM HIS RADIO JOB, HE TOOK THE FAMILY TO MARTHA'S PARENTS IN WACO, THEN WENT ON HIS WAY. HE'D GET THEM MOVED AS SOON AS HE COULD.

WILLIE REALLY WANTED TO MAKE AN HONEST GO OF IT. NO MORE DAY JOBS, DISTRACTIONS, OR EXCUSES. HE WAS GOING FULL SPEED AHEAD INTO THE NASHVILLE MACHINE — MUSIC CITY — AND HE'D SOON SEE IF HE MEASURED UP AS MUCH AS HE THOUGHT.

CHAPTER 4

★ GRINDING AWAY ★

WHEN WILLIE FINALLY ARRIVED IN HIS BEAT-UP BUICK, IT WAS AS IF THE CAR HAD FULFILLED ITS EARTHLY DUTIES — IT DIED ALMOST IMMEDIATELY.

WILLIE LEFT THE CAR BY THE SIDE OF THE ROAD, AND WALKED THE REST OF THE WAY INTO TOWN.

SUCCESS IN NASHVILLE DIDN'T COME WITHOUT HARDSHIP FOR WILLIE. IN THOSE FIRST FEW WEEKS IN NASHVILLE, HE WAS PEDDLING SONGS EVERY DAY, AND SITTING IN TOOTSIE'S WITH HIS STOMACH GROWLING BECAUSE HE COULDN'T EVEN PUT ENOUGH MONEY TOGETHER FOR A MEAL.

TOOTSIE'S ORCHID LOUNGE WAS ACROSS THE ALLEY FROM THE RYMAN AUDITORIUM, HOME OF THE GRAND OLE OPRY.

IT BECAME A NATURAL MEETING PLACE FOR MOVERS AND SHAKERS IN THE NASHVILLE MUSIC SCENE.

THE BACK ROOM OF TOOTSIE'S BECAME A NATURAL SAFE PLACE FOR SINGERS AND SONGWRITERS TO CONGREGATE AND SHARE THEIR WORK WITH EACH OTHER. SOME MUSICIANS WOULD LEAVE THEIR INSTRUMENTS AND AMPS THERE ALL THE TIME.

A FEW WEEKS IN, WILLIE AND A FEW OTHER SONGWRITERS WERE TALKING IN THAT BACK ROOM, AND HANK COCHRAN WALKED IN. HANK HAD JUST WRITTEN 'I FALL TO PIECES' WITH A MAN NAMED HARLAND HOWARD. THE ROOM TOOK NOTICE RIGHT AWAY.

WILLIE, HOWEVER, DIDN'T KNOW WHO HANK WAS JUST YET — AND THE OTHER SINGERS WERE TOO NERVOUS TO SHARE ANYTHING WHILE HANK WAS THERE.

WILLIE STEPPED UP AND PLAYED A FEW SONGS — 'TOUCH ME,' 'NIGHT LIFE' AND 'FUNNY HOW TIME SLIPS AWAY.'

HANK WAS VISIBLY IMPRESSED, AND OFFERED WILLIE A PUBLISHING CONTRACT WITH HIS COMPANY— PAMPER MUSIC.

WILLIE MADE THE TRIP WITH HANK TO GOODLETTSVILLE -
ABOUT TWENTY MILES NORTH OF NASHVILLE, WHERE HE
MET AND PLAYED HIS SONGS FOR HAL SMITH, OWNER OF
PAMPER MUSIC. HANK WAS ONE OF ITS STAR WRITERS.

ACCORDING TO HANK COCHRAN, HAL THOUGHT WILLIE
WAS A GREAT TALENT, BUT COULDN'T AFFORD TO HIRE
HIM JUST THEN.

HOWEVER, HANK HAD JUST TAKEN A RAISE OF FIFTY DOLLARS
A WEEK. HE TOOK HAL SMITH ASIDE A FEW DAYS LATER, AND
PROPOSED A COMPROMISE.

IF I GIVE UP MY RAISE,
WOULD YOU HIRE WILLIE
FOR THAT AMOUNT?

SURE, IF
YOU'RE WILLING
TO DO IT.

WILLIE PUT TOGETHER ENOUGH CASH TO SECURE A THREE
ROOM TRAILER IN THE FAMOUS DUNN'S TRAILER PARK. THERE
WAS A SIGN OUT FRONT - 'TRAILERS FOR SALE OR RENT.'

THESE WORDS LATER BECAME THE OPENING LYRICS IN
ROGER MILLER'S HIT SONG 'KING OF THE ROAD.'

WHEN HANK COCHRAN SHOWED UP AT WILLIE'S NEW HOME,
HE TOLD HIM THE GOOD NEWS. BY THIS POINT, MARTHA AND
THE KIDS HAD MOVED IN AS WELL. MARTHA HAD STARTED
WAITRESSING AT TOOTSIE'S BY THAT POINT AS WELL.

WILLIE! I CHANGED HAL'S
MIND. YOU'RE IN AT PAMPER!
CONGRATULATIONS, PAL.

ARE YOU
KIDDIN'?

THIS JOB FELT LIKE THE FIRST BIT OF GOOD NEWS
WILLIE HAD EVER HEARD IN HIS ENTIRE CAREER THUS
FAR. EVERYONE IN THAT LITTLE TRAILER FELT THE
SIGNIFICANCE.

WILLIE TOOK THE WORK OF SONGWRITER SERIOUSLY,
AND IN THAT OFFICE IN GOODLETTSVILLE, HE WASTED
NO TIME AT ALL.

ONE DAY WILLIE WAS HAVING SOME TROUBLE PUTTING SOMETHING TOGETHER, AND CALLED HANK TO BOUNCE A FEW IDEAS OFF OF. BEFORE LONG, HANK HAD TO TAKE A PHONE CALL.

IN THAT SHORT TIME HANK STEPPED OUT, WILLIE'S MUSE STRUCK HIM IN AN ODD BUT FRUITFUL WAY. HE'D BEEN STARING AT THE WALLS, QUITE LITERALLY, SEARCHING FOR INSPIRATION...

AND A SONG CALLED 'HELLO WALLS' FLOWED OUT OF WIL-LIE'S HEAD AND ONTO A PIECE OF STRAY CARDBOARD.

A FEW NIGHTS LATER, HANK AND WILLIE WENT DOWN TO TOOTSIE'S BACK ROOM, AND WILLIE PLAYED THE SONG FOR FARON YOUNG.

FARON LIKED IT SO MUCH, HE ASKED WILLIE TO TEACH HIM THE SONG, ALONG WITH ANOTHER SONG WILLIE HAD WRITTEN CALLED 'CONGRATULATIONS.'

YOUNG DECIDED TO RECORD 'HELLO WALLS' WITH 'CONGRATULATIONS' AS THE B-SIDE FOR CAPITAL RECORDS IN 1961. BEFORE THE SINGLE WAS RELEASED, WILLIE TRIED TO SELL HIM THE PUBLISHING RIGHTS FOR $500.

FARON REFUSED – AND INSTEAD HE OFFERED WILLIE A LOAN OF $500, ON THE CONDITION THAT HE NOT SELL THE SONG TO ANYONE.

'HELLO WALLS,' THE SAD SONG ABOUT LONELINESS, REACHED NUMBER 1 ON THE COUNTRY SINGLES CHARTS, AND STAYED THERE FOR 9 WEEKS.

THIS WEEK	ONE WEEK	TWO WEEK	THREE WE	Ⓢ	Indicates that version is av
				TITLE	Artist,
①	4	9	15	HELLO WALLS...	Faron
②	1	1	2	WALK ON BY...	Ler

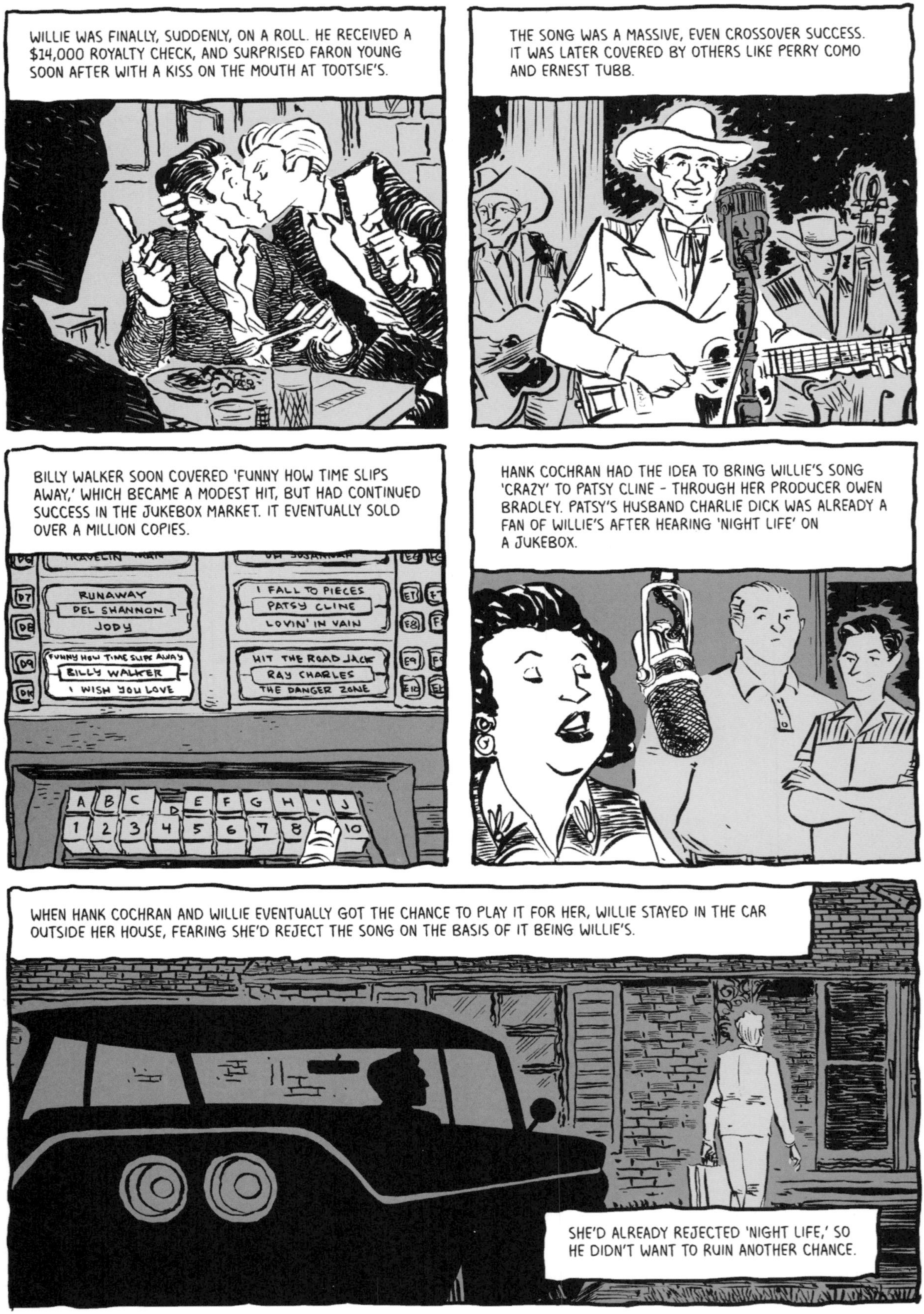
WILLIE WAS FINALLY, SUDDENLY, ON A ROLL. HE RECEIVED A $14,000 ROYALTY CHECK, AND SURPRISED FARON YOUNG SOON AFTER WITH A KISS ON THE MOUTH AT TOOTSIE'S.
THE SONG WAS A MASSIVE, EVEN CROSSOVER SUCCESS. IT WAS LATER COVERED BY OTHERS LIKE PERRY COMO AND ERNEST TUBB.
BILLY WALKER SOON COVERED 'FUNNY HOW TIME SLIPS AWAY,' WHICH BECAME A MODEST HIT, BUT HAD CONTINUED SUCCESS IN THE JUKEBOX MARKET. IT EVENTUALLY SOLD OVER A MILLION COPIES.
RUNAWAY
DEL SHANNON
JODY
I FALL TO PIECES
PATSY CLINE
LOVIN' IN VAIN
FUNNY HOW TIME SLIPS AWAY
BILLY WALKER
I WISH YOU LOVE
HIT THE ROAD JACK
RAY CHARLES
THE DANGER ZONE
HANK COCHRAN HAD THE IDEA TO BRING WILLIE'S SONG 'CRAZY' TO PATSY CLINE - THROUGH HER PRODUCER OWEN BRADLEY. PATSY'S HUSBAND CHARLIE DICK WAS ALREADY A FAN OF WILLIE'S AFTER HEARING 'NIGHT LIFE' ON A JUKEBOX.
WHEN HANK COCHRAN AND WILLIE EVENTUALLY GOT THE CHANCE TO PLAY IT FOR HER, WILLIE STAYED IN THE CAR OUTSIDE HER HOUSE, FEARING SHE'D REJECT THE SONG ON THE BASIS OF IT BEING WILLIE'S.
SHE'D ALREADY REJECTED 'NIGHT LIFE,' SO HE DIDN'T WANT TO RUIN ANOTHER CHANCE.

PATSY LIKED THE SONG, BUT WASN'T ENTIRELY SURE IT WAS A GOOD FIT FOR HER.

HE'S SITTING OUT THERE IN THE CAR - TOO EMBARRASSED TO COME IN..

AND HANK LATER DESCRIBED THAT SHE "WENT OUT THERE AND DRUG HIS ASS IN AND HAD HIM SING IT TO HER UNTIL SHE LEARNED IT."

WELL, I'M GOING TO GET THAT LITTLE SON OF A BITCH!

PATSY EVENTUALLY RELENTED, AND RECORDED WHAT WAS TO BECOME ONE OF THE MOST FAMOUS JUKEBOX SONGS OF ALL TIME.

THE NELSON FAMILY HAD QUITE THE EVENTFUL YEAR IN 1961. WITH ONE OF HIS FIRST ROYALTY CHECKS, WILLIE BOUGHT MARTHA A 1959 CADILLAC, PREVIOUSLY OWNED BY RAY PRICE. REAL MONEY WAS STARTING TO COME INTO THEIR LIVES.

AT THE SAME TIME HOWEVER, THE MARRIAGE WAS FALLING APART. MARTHA HAD STARTED DRINKING WHILE WORKING AT TOOTSIE'S, AND WILLIE WAS WORKING MORE THAN EVER.

WHILE WILLIE'S SONGS WERE CLIMBING UP THE CHARTS, HE HAD HEARD THAT RAY PRICE WAS IN NEED OF A BASS PLAYER FOR HIS BAND.

RAY HAD TAKEN OVER HANK WILLIAMS' BAND AFTER HE DIED, AND WILLIE FELT STRONGLY ABOUT BEING A SMALL PART OF MUSIC HISTORY.

WILLIE DIDN'T PLAY BASS, BUT HE LEARNED VERY QUICKLY, OUT OF NECESSITY.

YOU PLAY ANY BASS, WILLIE?

DOESN'T EVERYBODY?

SO WILLIE BECAME ONE OF RAY PRICE'S CHEROKEE COWBOYS - THE FORMER BACKING BAND OF THE LATE GREAT HANK WILLIAMS.

WHILE THINGS WERE GOING WELL WITH RAY PRICE AND THE BAND, WILLIE'S MARRIAGE TO MARTHA WAS FALLING APART.

ON MORE THAN A FEW OCCASIONS, HE'D USE HIS SONGWRITING MONEY TO THROW PARTIES IN HIS HOTEL SUITES ON THE ROAD.

THERE WERE MANY ARGUMENTS AND ACCUSATIONS, BUT IT CAME TO A HEAD ONE NIGHT AT TOOTSIE'S WHEN MARTHA BECAME SO ANGRY, SHE STARTED THROWING WHISKEY GLASSES AT WILLIE.

HE MANAGED TO DODGE THEM, BUT HANK COCHRAN'S FACE GOT CAUGHT IN THE CROSSFIRE. WILLIE HAD TO TAKE HIM TO THE HOSPITAL IN THE MIDDLE OF THE NIGHT.

IN 1962, WILLIE AND MARTHA'S MARRIAGE FINALLY CAME TO AN END.

WILLIE COULDN'T QUITE MANAGE TO STAY FAITHFUL ON THE ROAD, OR IN THE STUDIOS OF NASHVILLE. HE AND SHIRLEY COLLIE, BOTH MARRIED TO OTHER PEOPLE, BEGAN AN AFFAIR.

THEY RECORDED TWO VERY TELLING DUETS NAMED 'WILLINGLY,' AND 'CHAIN OF LOVE,' WHICH DESCRIBED THEIR AFFAIR AND MARRIAGES.

BUT EVEN BEFORE THAT RELATIONSHIP BEGAN, WILLIE AND MARTHA'S MARRIAGE WAS, AT THAT POINT, IRREPARABLE.

MARTHA SOON TOOK THE KIDS, AND THAT BIG BLACK CADILLAC, ALL THE WAY TO LAS VEGAS, WHERE SHE FILED FOR DIVORCE. SHE AND THE KIDS FOUND A SMALL APARTMENT.

FOR A TIME, THE ONLY WAY WILLIE WILLIE WOULD SEE THE KIDS WAS WHEN HE CAME THROUGH TOWN ON A GIG. FOR SOME REASON, WILLIE DECIDED TO SEND SHIRLEY TO GO PICK THEM UP.

MARTHA REACTED AS WELL AS SHE COULD'VE.

DON'T EVER COME BACK!! AND YOU TELL THAT FUCKIN' WILLIE NELSON HE'LL **NEVER** SEE HIS KIDS AGAIN!!

IF HE WANTS HIS KIDS, HE BETTER BE MAN ENOUGH TO COME AND GET THEM HIMSELF AND DON'T SEND HIS **FUCKIN' WHORE** NEXT TIME!

BY THIS POINT, THE FULL LENGTH SOLO ALBUM WILLIE HAD RECORDED FOR LIBERTY RECORDS HAD BEEN RELEASED.

IT WAS CALLED '...AND THEN I WROTE.'

THE SONGS WERE MOSTLY WILLIE'S, EXCEPT FOR ONE BY HANK COCHRAN. THEY WERE RECORDED IN NASHVILLE AND NEARBY LIBERTY'S HEADQUARTERS IN L.A. OVER THE COURSE OF 1961.

THE RECORD CERTAINLY DIDN'T SET THE WORLD ON FIRE, SALES-WISE. BEING ON THE LIBERTY LABEL, HOWEVER, ALLOWED HIM TO TOUR AS A SOLO ACT, WHICH WAS ALWAYS WILLIE'S GOAL.

FOR A SONGWRITER, HOWEVER CONTENT YOU MIGHT BE, THE PAIN FROM THE PAST WILL SHINE THROUGH, THE NEXT TIME YOU WRITE A SONG FROM YOUR HEART.

WILLIE CHANNELED THE PAIN OF THE BREAKUP WITH MARTHA INTO A SONG CALLED 'THE HEALING HANDS OF TIME.'

*They're working while I'm missing you
Those healing hands of time
And soon they'll be dismissing you
from this heart of mine*

WILLIE HAD FALLEN FOR SHIRLEY COLLIE HEAD OVER HEELS, AND WASN'T SHY ABOUT PROPOSING MARRIAGE EVERY CHANCE HE COULD, NOW THAT THE MARRIAGE TO MARTHA WAS OFFICIALLY OVER.

SHIRLEY EVENTUALLY FELT THE SAME, THOUGH IT TOOK TIME.

IN LATE 1963, THE COUPLE WANTED TO SETTLE DOWN AND FIND A PROPER HOME, AND THEY FOUND ONE – A HOUSE ON GREER ROAD, IN THE TOWN OF RIDGETOP, TENNESSEE.

IT WAS THEIR DREAM HOUSE. COMPLETE WITH A FARM ATTACHED.

THE SAME DAY THEY FOUND THAT HOUSE, PRESIDENT KENNEDY WAS SHOT.

WILLIE DIDN'T RUN THE FARM HIMSELF, AS THAT WOULD'VE BEEN A DISASTER. THERE WAS A 'WHISKEY-DRINKING HORSE TRADER' NAMED MR. HUGHES ALONG WITH HIS WIFE RUBY.

HE WAS IN CHARGE OF THE DAY-TO-DAY, ALONG WITH BUYING CATTLE AND HORSES.

AFTER IT BECAME KNOWN HOW MUCH SPACE WILLIE HAD GOTTEN A HOLD OF, MORE FAMILY MEMBERS CAME TO STAY. FIRST, IT WAS THE KIDS.

LANA, SUSIE AND BILLIE WERE SENT TO LIVE AT RIDGETOP, BECAUSE MARTHA WAS GOING THROUGH THE END OF ANOTHER MARRIAGE.

THEN IT WAS WILLIE'S FATHER, IRA AND HIS WIFE LORRAINE, WILLIE'S STEPBROTHERS DOYLE AND CHARLES, FOLLOWED BY SISTER BOBBIE AND HER THREE SONS.

QUITE THE PLACE YOU'VE GOT HERE, SON.

THE HORSES ARE BEAUTIFUL, WILLIE!

AS MORE MONEY CAME IN FROM HIS SONGS, THE MORE LAND WILLIE BOUGHT. HE WAS ENJOYING LIFE ON THE FARM, AND AT ONE POINT HE GAINED THIRTY POUNDS FROM ENJOYING A BIT TOO MUCH OF THE FRESH FOOD.

HE STARTED TO RESEMBLE ONE OF HIS OVERFED PIGS, SO HE HIRED A KUNG-FU MASTER TO HELP HIM GET BACK IN SHAPE.

AND BECAUSE LIBERTY RECORDS GAVE UP ON WILLIE IN 1964, AFTER TWO UNDERPERFORMING RECORDS, HE DECIDED TO REACH OUT TO CHET ATKINS AT RCA NASHVILLE.

HOWEVER, WILLIE'S INSTINCTS ULTIMATELY LED HIM TO FRED FOSTER AT MONUMENT RECORDS INSTEAD, WHO PRODUCED ROY ORBISON - ANOTHER ARTIST FROM TEXAS WHO WAS DIFFICULT TO PIN DOWN, MUSICALLY - MUCH LIKE WILLIE.

BY ALL ACCOUNTS, A MONUMENT RECORDS-SIGNED WILLIE WOULD BE ABLE TO SHINE AS HIS TRUE ARTISTIC SELF, AND NOT BE BOUND BY TYPICAL NASHVILLE EXPECTATIONS.

EVERYONE INVOLVED WAS OPTIMISTIC - AND AN AD AGENCY EVEN CAME ABOARD TO PLACE A FULL PAGE AD CAMPAIGN INSIDE THE PAGES OF BILLBOARD MAGAZINE.

THE AD WAS THEMED LIKE A CORONATION - AS IF WILLIE WERE THE NEW KING OF COUNTRY MUSIC. BUT WHEN THE DAY CAME, AND THE AD WAS TO BE IN BILLBOARD - WILLIE OPENED UP THE MAGAZINE AND SAW NOT HIMSELF, BUT LLOYD PRICE, ANOTHER ONE OF MONUMENT'S ARTISTS.

IT WAS LATER CHALKED UP TO A MISUNDERSTANDING, BUT WILLIE WAS HEARTBROKEN. HE NEVER FINISHED RECORDING THE MONUMENT ALBUM, AND SOON SIGNED WITH CHET ATKINS AT RCA VICTOR.

ONE SILVER LINING OF WILLIE'S RELATIONSHIP WITH FRED FOSTER AND MONUMENT RECORDS, HOWEVER, WAS PLACING ONE OF WILLIE'S RECENT SONGS, THE CHRISTMAS-THEMED 'PRETTY PAPER,' WITH ROY ORBISON.

DURING THE MONUMENT-TO-RCA TRANSITION, WILLIE RECEIVED AN INVITATION TO APPEAR ON THE GRAND OLE OPRY, WHICH BROUGHT QUITE A BIT OF PRESTIGE AND RECOGNITION.

BUT FOR WILLIE, AS EXCITING AS IT WAS TO BE ON THAT LEGENDARY STAGE - THE RYMAN AUDITORIUM - IT ALSO MEANT MORE RESTRICTIONS AND MORE OBLIGATIONS.

IT MEANT LESS TIME TO PLAY HIS OWN SHOWS ON THE ROAD, AND LESS MONEY AS A RESULT.

AFTER GIVING IT SOME TIME, WILLIE ULTIMATELY QUIT THE OPRY, BUT CONTINUED TO APPEAR ON TELEVISION OCCASIONALLY - ON THE ERNEST TUBB SHOW, AS WELL AS PORTER WAGONER'S.

WILLIE'S CALM CONFIDENCE DURING THESE APPEARANCES EARNED THE RESPECT OF THE MUSICIANS ON THE SHOW AS WELL AS THE VIEWERS AT HOME.

ALTHOUGH HE WAS STARTING TO FEEL LIKE HIMSELF IN SOME WAYS, HIS RECORDS AT RCA CONTINUED TO PUT HIM IN THE NASHVILLE BUTTON-DOWN MOLD.

TO HIS DETRIMENT, HE PUT TOO MUCH FAITH IN CHET ATKINS' HANDS. NEITHER OF HIS RCA RELEASES SET THE MUSIC WORLD ON FIRE. EVEN THOUGH CHET TALKED ABOUT MARKETING WILLIE TO THE MAINSTREAM, RCA CONTINUED TO DO MORE OF THE SAME.

AROUND THIS TIME, WILLIE STARTED TO BEFRIEND A FEW PEOPLE THAT SEEMED TO CEMENT, BUT ALSO REFLECT WILLIE'S REBELLIOUS NATURE - WHEN IT CAME TO HIS MUSIC.

ONE OF THOSE PEOPLE WAS WAYLON JENNINGS - ANOTHER HARD-TO-CLASSIFY TEXAS-BORN SINGER WHO WAS ABOUT TO HEAD TO NASHVILLE. BUT AFTER MEETING HIM AND SEEING HIM PERFORM - ADVISED WAYLON TO STAY AWAY FROM MUSIC CITY ALTOGETHER.

NASHVILLE WILL WANT TO MOLD YOU, AND YOU DON'T NEED MOLDING. NASHVILLE WILL WANT TO CLEAN YOU UP, AND YOU DON'T NEED CLEANING.

BUT WAYLON DIDN'T FOLLOW THE ADVICE, AND SOON SIGNED WITH CHET ATKINS AT RCA NASHVILLE.

SOMEONE ELSE WHO SEEMED LIKE A KINDRED SPIRIT WAS CHARLEY PRIDE, A GREAT COUNTRY SINGER, WHO ALSO HAPPENED TO BE BLACK.

NATURALLY, THERE WAS A LOT OF PUSHBACK FROM COUNTRY MUSIC FANS ABOUT AN AFRICAN-AMERICAN SINGER. ALL DOUBT, HOWEVER, WAS ERASED AFTER THEY HEARD HIM SING.

AT ONE POINT, CHARLEY JOINED WILLIE'S TOUR, ALONG WITH HANK COCHRAN AND JOHNNY BUSH.

AND ON ONE PARTICULAR MEMORABLE EVENING, PLAYING A SHOW IN DALLAS, WILLIE INTRODUCED CHARLEY, AND PROCEEDED TO KISS HIM SQUARE ON THE MOUTH.

THIS LIKELY RUFFLED SOME FEATHERS, BEING IN THE SOUTHERN PART OF THE COUNTRY.

ON THE ROAD, WILLIE FELT MORE AND MORE FREE, WHILE AT THE SAME TIME, HE FELT THE SAME OLD RESTRICTIONS AND PUSHBACK FROM CHET ATKINS AT RCA NASHVILLE.

IN A LAST DITCH EFFORT, IN THE LATE 60'S, RECORD COMPANIES TRIED 'REPACKAGING' COUNTRY WITH ELEMENTS OF FOLK MUSIC – IN TERMS OF MARKETING AND CONTENT.

THIS HAPPENED AROUND THE SAME TIME BOB DYLAN WAS EXPERIMENTING WITH COUNTRY.

WILLIE AGAIN WENT ALONG WITH RCA, AND DIDN'T SEEM TO MIND – HE LIKED THE SONGS HE WAS COVERING, AND DIDN'T THINK IT WAS SUCH A HUGE LEAP. HE RECORDED SONGS LIKE 'JONI MITCHELL'S 'BOTH SIDES NOW' AND 'EVERYBODY'S TALKIN' FROM MIDNIGHT COWBOY.

IN 1969, THE BALDWIN GUITAR WILLIE HAD BEEN USING, SINCE SWITCHING OVER FROM FENDER ELECTRIC GUITARS, SUSTAINED A BROKEN NECK.

HE FOUND A GORGEOUS SOUNDING MARTIN CLASSICAL GUITAR MADE OF ROSEWOOD TO REPLACE IT, AND HAD THE GUITAR CUSTOMIZED IN NASHVILLE TO INCORPORATE THE ELECTRIC PICKUP FROM THE BALDWIN.

HE NAMED THE NEW GUITAR 'TRIGGER,' AFTER ROY ROGERS' HORSE.

IT WAS THANKSGIVING, WHEN WILLIE AND SHIRLEY'S RELATIONSHIP CAME TO AN ABRUPT, BUT NOT ALTOGETHER SURPRISING END.

SHIRLEY CONFRONTED WILLIE AT HOME - AT THEIR GREER ROAD HOUSE IN RIDGETOP - WITH WHAT APPEARED TO BE A HOSPITAL BILL.

THE BILL LISTED CHARGES INCURRED FOR THE BIRTH OF A BABY GIRL, PAULA CARLENE, BORN OCTOBER 27, 1969, TO A MRS. CONNIE NELSON.

WHO IS THIS **CONNIE?** WHOSE **BABY** IS THIS?

WHAT THE **GODDAMN** HELL IS **GOING** ON??

CONNIE KOEPKE HAD BEEN WILLIE'S GIRLFRIEND FOR YEARS WHILE ON THE ROAD.

WILLIE MADE SURE HE WAS THERE TO DO THE PAPERWORK, BUT DIDN'T THINK THROUGH WHERE THEY WERE GOING TO SEND THE BILL. HE LISTED THE GREER ROAD ADDRESS.

AND IN WINTER 1969, SHIRLEY MOVED OUT. SHORTLY THEREAFTER, CONNIE AND THE BABY MOVED IN. WILLIE'S FAMILY AND HOME LIFE CONTINUED TO CHANGE. HIS MUSIC CAREER, AS FULFILLING AS SOME PARTS WERE, SEEMED TO BE AT A CROSSROADS.

CHAPTER 5

★ AUSTIN, TEXAS ★

IN DECEMBER 1970, WILLIE WROTE A SONG CALLED "WHAT CAN YOU DO TO ME NOW?" WITH HANK COCHRAN.

IT'S ALMOST AS IF HE WAS INVITING MORE BAD LUCK AND HEARTACHE WITH THAT PROPHETIC SONG, AFTER AN ALREADY TUMULTUOUS DECADE.

THE NEXT DAY, WILLIE WAS ATTENDING A CHRISTMAS PARTY AT A CLUB IN NASHVILLE WHEN HE GOT THE CALL.

UNCLE WILLIE! YOU GOTTA GET **UP** HERE! YOU GOTTA COME RIGHT NOW!

YOUR HOUSE IS ON **FIRE! EVERYTHING'S** BURNING DOWN!

TAKE MY OLD CAR AND PARK IT IN THE GARAGE!

ARE YOU KIDDING?

DEAD SERIOUS! INSURANCE IS GONNA PAY FOR ALL THIS - MIGHT AS WELL HAVE A NEW CAR!

WHEN WILLIE ARRIVED, HE RACED INTO THE HOUSE, DESPITE PROTESTS FROM THE FIREMEN - AND RETRIEVED TWO GUITAR CASES FROM HIS BEDROOM.

ONE WAS HIS PRIZED MARTIN GUITAR TRIGGER...

...AND THE OTHER CONTAINED TWO POUNDS OF COLUMBIAN POT.

IT'S ALL GONE, WILLIE. IT'S ALL GONE UP IN SMOKE.

ALL THAT'S GONE IS MATERIAL STUFF. OUR SPIRIT AIN'T GONE. OUR SPIRIT'S STRONGER THAN EVER.

THE INSURANCE PAYOUT WAS SUBSTANTIAL ENOUGH FOR WILLIE AND HIS FAMILY TO REBUILD THE HOME - BUT THAT WOULDN'T HAPPEN OVERNIGHT.

IN THE MEANTIME, THOUGH, HE THOUGHT GOING BACK TO TEXAS FOR A BIT WAS A GOOD PLAN.

THE FAMILY FOUND A RANCH NEAR SAN ANTONIO THAT WAS SHUT DOWN FOR THE SEASON...

AND A FRIEND OF WILLIE'S ARRANGED FOR THEM TO STAY THERE.

THIS WAS A TIME OF DEEP REFLECTION FOR WILLIE.

READING SCRIPTURE, AS WELL AS THE WORK OF KHALIL GIBRAN.

THIS INTERNAL DIALOGUE EVENTUALLY LED TO WILLIE'S RELIGIOUS-TINGED CONCEPT ALBUM...

Nelson

Yesterday's Wine

'YESTERDAY'S WINE.'

UNFORTUNATELY THE CONCEPT WAS LOST ON THE RECORD COMPANY.

IT'S YOUR FUCKIN' WORST ALBUM TO DATE!

APPARENTLY A RELIGIOUS, PHILOSOPHICAL JOURNEY WAS TOO HIGH MINDED FOR THE GENERAL PUBLIC, EVEN IF IT DID INCLUDE A CLASSIC LIKE 'FAMILY BIBLE' AS ONE OF ITS CENTERPIECES.

THESE ARE MY SONGS. I LIKE 'EM. I'M PROUD OF 'EM. AND THAT'S IT.

THE RECORD BOMBED, BUT ANOTHER SONG, 'ME AND PAUL' ENDED UP BECOMING A CLASSIC YEARS LATER.

Welcome to Nashville

THIS TIME OF QUIET REFLECTION, POSITIVE THINKING, AND DEEP PHILOSOPHICAL QUESTIONING ALSO COINCIDED WITH WILLIE'S GROWING APPRECIATION OF MARIJUANA.

ALTHOUGH HE BEGAN PLAYING THE JOHNNY BUSH-WRITTEN 'WHISKEY RIVER' TO OPEN EVERY SHOW AROUND THIS TIME...

WHISKEY RIVER TAKE MY MIIIIIINNND...

WILLIE NOW SAW THE BENEFITS OF THE CANNABIS PLANT, AS WELL AS THE CULTURE OF LOVE AND COMMUNITY THAT SURROUNDED IT.

WHEN THE FAMILY'S HOUSE IN TENNESSEE WAS FINALLY REBUILT, WILLIE CONTINUED TO FOLLOW HIS GUT AND STAY IN TEXAS. HOUSTON WAS THE CITY WILLIE HAD IN MIND, BUT IT SOON BECAME CLEAR...THAT AUSTIN WOULD BE HIS NEW **HOME**.

NOT ONLY WAS THERE A GROWING COUNTERCULTURE AND EXCITING MUSIC SCENE, BUT ALSO FAMILY. SISTER BOBBIE HAD BEEN LIVING THERE WITH HER BOYS...

AND WOULD SOON JOIN WILLIE'S BAND AGAIN.

AUSTIN WAS GOING TO BE WILLIE'S CITY.

AND IN LATE 1972, WILLIE AND HIS BAND PLAYED THE FAMOUS ARMADILLO WORLD HEADQUARTERS FOR THE FIRST TIME.

I'M CRAZY FOR FEEEEELINGG SO LONELYYY...

BY THE EARLY SEVENTIES, WILLIE SEEMED TO BE MORE COMFORTABLE BEING HIMSELF, AND THAT WAS HELPED ALONG THE PATH BY PEOPLE LIKE JERRY WEXLER OF ATLANTIC RECORDS.

JERRY SEEMED TO UNDERSTAND WHERE WILLIE WAS COMING FROM ARTISTICALLY – AND THAT THE POTENTIAL WAS THERE FOR A SERIOUS BREAKTHROUGH.

WILLIE'S CONTRACT WITH RCA WAS UP, AND ATLANTIC CAME ALONG AT JUST THE RIGHT TIME.

WILLIE LISTENED TO HIS HEART AND INSTINCTS, AND IT LED HIM TO TAKE ON A SERIOUS GOSPEL-THEMED ALBUM CALLED 'THE TROUBLEMAKER.'

WILLIE GAINED COMPLETE ARTISTIC CONTROL IN HIS NEW LABEL PARTNERSHIP. GONE WERE THE FORCED POLISHINGS OF THE NASHVILLE MACHINE. THIS RECORD WAS RECORDED IN NEW YORK CITY, WHICH PROVIDED A FRESH CONTRAST FROM NASHVILLE.

BOBBIE NELSON ALSO PLAYED ON THE RECORD – THE FIRST TIME THE TWO SIBLINGS HAD RECORDED TOGETHER.

WEXLER WAS PLEASED BY THE NEW ALBUM, AND ENCOURAGED WILLIE TO DO ANOTHER ONE RIGHT AWAY – THIS TIME GOING IN ANOTHER, MORE REBELLIOUS DIRECTION.

WHY DON'T YOU STAY AROUND AND CUT SOME MORE TUNES?

THE RESULTING CONCEPT RECORD AND TITLE TRACK WERE CALLED 'SHOTGUN WILLIE.' THE TITLE REFERENCED AN INCIDENT THAT INVOLVED WILLIE, HIS DAUGHTER LANA, AND HER THEN BOYFRIEND WHO'D BEEN HITTING HER.

THAT SONG IS SO DUMB IT'S BOUND TO BE A BIG HIT!

HA!

'SHOTGUN WILLIE' WAS SOON NELSON'S BIGGEST SELLING ALBUM TO DATE.

SEEING THE SUCCESS OF AN OUTDOOR MUSIC FESTIVAL LIKE THE DRIPPING SPRINGS REUNION GAVE WILLIE AN IDEA OF HIS OWN -TO CREATE AN EVENT LIKE THAT HIMSELF.

AND IN 1973, WILLIE PUT ON HIS FIRST FOURTH OF JULY PICNIC, IN TEXAS, WITH AS MANY FRIENDS AND MUSICAL ACTS AS HE COULD BOOK.

WHEN HE WAS TALKING ABOUT THE IDEA OF THE PICNIC, HIS TRUSTED FRIEND LEON RUSSELL TOLD HIM...

YOU BRING THE REDNECKS, WILLIE, AND I'LL BRING THE HIPPIES.

FINANCIALLY, THE FESTIVAL DIDN'T MAKE A PROFIT, BUT ATTENDANCE WAS OUTSTANDING, AND BRINGING TOGETHER DIFFERENT KINDS OF PEOPLE FOR THE LOVE OF MUSIC WAS SOMETHING WILLIE WOULD ALWAYS ENCOURAGE.

JUST TWO DAYS LATER, ON JULY 6TH, WILLIE'S DAUGHTER AMY LEE WAS BORN. HIS FOURTH CHILD, AND SECOND WITH CONNIE.

WILLIE'S NEXT ALBUM, 'PHASES AND STAGES,' WAS A CONCEPT ALBUM ABOUT A COUPLE'S DIVORCE. SIDE A WAS THE WOMAN'S PERSPECTIVE, AND SIDE B WAS THE MAN'S ACCOUNT OF THINGS.

IT WAS ONE OF WILLIE'S MOST SINCERE AND HEARTFELT WORKS.

WHEN WILLIE PLAYED THE SONGS IN PERSON FOR JERRY WEXLER, HE WAS BROUGHT TO TEARS

THIS PERIOD WAS AN ERA OF FREEDOM FOR WILLIE AND HIS CLOSE KNIT GROUP OF PEERS, LIKE WAYLON JENNINGS.

THE MEDIA AT THE TIME - MORE SPECIFICALLY GOSSIP COLUMNIST HAZEL SMITH - SETTLED ON THE TERM 'OUTLAW MUSIC' AND THE ONE MAIN THING THESE MUSICIANS HAD IN COMMON WAS THEIR NEED TO BREAK OUT OF THE RIGID NASHVILLE MOLD OF COUNTRY MUSIC.

AS WELL AS EVERYTHING WAS GOING, SOMETHING HAD TO GIVE. JERRY WEXLER SOON INFORMED WILLIE THAT ATLANTIC WAS CLOSING THEIR NASHVILLE OFFICES AND OVERALL COUNTRY MUSIC DIVISION.

I'M URGING YOU AND NEIL RESHEN TO FIND ANOTHER LABEL WITH A STRONG NASHVILLE OPERATION.

THEY WERE BOTH HEARTBROKEN. WEXLER LET WILLIE OUT OF HIS CONTRACT, EVEN THOUGH HE HAD TWO MORE RELEASES STIPULATED IN IT.

HIS NEW LABEL TURNED OUT TO BE COLUMBIA RECORDS

THIS NEW DEAL GAVE HIM COMPLETE ARTISTIC CONTROL - AND THAT FREEDOM EXTENDED TO EVEN THE PHYSICAL RECORD JACKETS AS WELL. FOR THE FIRST TIME, HE WAS ALSO ALLOWED TO USE HIS OWN BAND IN THE STUDIO.

WILLIE'S FIRST RELEASE THROUGH COLUMBIA WAS 'RED HEADED STRANGER.' HE HAD SUNG THE SONG TO HIS CHILDREN EVER SINCE THEY WERE YOUNG, AND CONNIE HAD THE IDEA TO EXPAND IT INTO YET ANOTHER CONCEPT ALBUM.

CONNIE AND WILLIE COOKED UP THE IDEA WHILE ON A LONG DRIVE. IT WOULD BE A WESTERN THEME, ABOUT LOST LOVE AND VIOLENCE.

THE RECORDING SESSIONS WERE SPARSE IN SOUND - IN THAT THEY HAD NO SIGNS OF NASHVILLE-TYPE POLISH. WILLIE HAD TO FIGHT A BIT WITH THE LABEL TO KEEP IT THAT WAY. SOME REMARKED IT SOUNDED LIKE AN ALBUM OF DEMOS.

'BLUE EYES CRYING IN THE RAIN' MADE IT ONTO THE ALBUM, WHICH WAS WRITTEN BY FRED ROSE. IT WAS RELEASED AS A SINGLE FROM THE NEW RECORD, AND IT QUICKLY WENT TO NUMBER ONE ON THE CHARTS. A BONAFIDE SMASH.

ALTHOUGH THE 'OUTLAW' MOVEMENT WAS AN IMPORTANT WAY TO SEPARATE THEMSELVES FROM THE BUTTON-DOWN NASHVILLE ESTABLISHMENT, THE MEDIA KEPT PUSHING THE NARRATIVE. IT GOT TO BE A BIT TIRESOME FOR WAYLON IN PARTICULAR.

DON'T YOU THINK THIS OUTLAW BIT HAS GOTTEN OUT OF HAND?

WAYLON, WILLIE, JESSI COLTER, AND TOMPALL GLASER RELEASED A COMPILATION ALBUM CALLED 'WANTED! THE OUTLAWS' ON RCA VICTOR IN 1976. IT WENT ON TO BECOME ONE OF THE BEST-SELLING COUNTRY ALBUMS OF THE SEVENTIES.

NOT ONLY WERE WILLIE'S ALBUMS SELLING, BUT HIS CONCERTS AND FESTIVALS KEPT GOING AT A LIGHTNING PACE AS WELL.

THE 1975 PICNIC WELCOMED OVER 50,000 ATTENDEES, AND TRAFFIC WAS BLOCKED IN AND OUT OF LIBERTY, TEXAS, WHERE IT WAS HELD. JULY 4TH, 1975 WAS DECLARED 'WILLIE NELSON DAY' BY THE TEXAS SENATE.

THE 1976 BICENTENNIAL FOURTH OF JULY PICNIC WAS HELD IN GONZALES, TEXAS, AND WAS EXPANDED TO A THREE DAY FESTIVAL.

WILLIE WAS NOW RIDING A WAVE OF SUCCESS FEW COULD'VE PREDICTED.

IN 1977, WILLIE WAS ON TOUR WITH HIS OLD FRIEND HANK COCHRAN. THEY TOOK A BREAK FROM THE BUSY SCHEDULE TO DO SOME FISHING ON HANK'S BOAT IN THE BAHAMAS.

WHEN THEY ARRIVED, A CUSTOMS AGENT MET THEM WITH THEIR LUGGAGE.

WILLIE HAD FORGOTTEN HE'D STASHED AWAY A SMALL AMOUNT OF WEED IN A PAIR OF JEANS THAT MADE ITS WAY INTO THE SUITCASE. THE AGENT OPENED THE SUITCASE, AND THE JEANS HAPPENED TO BE RIGHT ON TOP.

WHAT'S THE PROBLEM?

THIS IS THE PROBLEM.

AND SOON WILLIE WAS TAKEN AWAY IN A VAN AND THROWN IN A CELL, AS HANK COCHRAN LOOKED ON.

EVEN THOUGH WILLIE HAD QUIT DRINKING BY THIS POINT, HANK CAME BACK TO VISIT HIM WITH A SIX PACK OF BEER. WILLIE HAD NOTHING ELSE TO DO, SO HE DRANK UNTIL HANK CAME BACK WITH THE BAIL MONEY.

WHEN HANK CAME BACK TO GET HIM OUT, WILLIE WAS COMPLETELY DRUNK.

WHOO HOOO!

WHEN THE SUNLIGHT HIT HIS FACE, WILLIE JUMPED OFF THE JAIL'S PORCH AND BROKE HIS LEFT FOOT – AND SPENT THE NEXT FIVE HOURS IN AN EMERGENCY ROOM.

TWO DAYS LATER, WITH A CAST ON HIS FOOT, HE PERFORMED FOR THE CARTERS AT THE WHITE HOUSE.

AND THAT NIGHT, THERE WAS A KNOCK ON HIS DOOR. WILLIE WAS GIVEN AN INSIDER'S TOUR OF THE HOUSE, AND SOON FOUND HIMSELF SMOKING A JOINT ON THE ROOF OF THAT FAMOUS RESIDENCE.

HOW THE **FUCK** DID I GET HERE?

CHAPTER 6

★ HONEYSUCKLE ROSE ★

AS THE SEVENTIES WERE DRAWING TO A CLOSE, WILLIE CONTINUED TO CEMENT HIS STATUS IN THE MAINSTREAM OF NOT ONLY COUNTRY MUSIC, BUT IN THE MAINSTREAM OF POP CULTURE AS WELL.

Ray, how can I win with Braille chess pieces? I can't **SEE**!

BY 1979, WILLIE WAS SEEING SEVERAL OF HIS RECENT ALBUMS REACHING PLATINUM STATUS.

HE AND WAYLON JENNINGS HAD RELEASED A SONG TOGETHER, 'MAMMAS DON'T LET YOUR BABIES GROW UP TO BE COWBOYS,' AND BOTH OF THEIR STARS WERE RISING WITH THE GENERAL PUBLIC.

RECORD EXECUTIVES AT WILLIE'S THEN CURRENT LABEL, COLUMBIA, WERE EAGER TO RELEASE NEW MATERIAL TO CAPITALIZE ON HIS RECENT CROSSOVER.

Plink Plink

it's wonderful it's wonderful so they tell me

IN HIS YOUTH, WILLIE LOVED THE SONGS OF FRANK SINATRA, AND ADMIRED THE WAY HE INTERPRETED COMPOSITIONS IN HIS SIGNATURE STYLE.

WILLIE DECIDED FOR HIS NEXT ALBUM, HE'D RECORD STANDARDS LIKE 'STARDUST,' 'BLUE SKIES,' 'GEORGIA ON MY MIND,' 'UNCHAINED MELODY,' AND OTHERS.

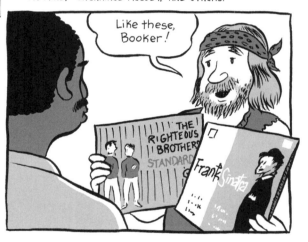

Like these, Booker!

THE RIGHTEOUS BROTHERS STANDARD

Frank Sinatra

THE RESULTING RELEASE, CALLED 'STARDUST,' WASN'T MET WITH MUCH ENTHUSIASM BY COLUMBIA RECORDS.

They're songs from a forgotten era! People don't want to hear songs they associate with their fathers or grandfathers!

Listen to **REASON**!

WILLIE'S MIND WAS ALREADY MADE UP. HE ALSO WENT AGAINST COLUMBIA'S ADVICE TO PUT HIMSELF ON THE ALBUM COVER. THE ARRANGEMENTS, LIKE RED HEADED STRANGER, WERE SPARSE AND GRITTY.

HE WANTED TO KEEP THEM THAT WAY.

I'm listening to my heart.

STARDUST WENT ON TO SELL MILLIONS, AND EVEN STAYED ON THE BILLBOARD CHARTS FOR OVER TEN YEARS.

THE SUCCESS OF THAT ALBUM GAVE WILLIE THE CONFIDENCE HE NEEDED TO STAND HIS GROUND WHEN IT CAME TO RECORD COMPANY PUSHBACK.

HE REALIZED HE SHOULD RELY ON HIS INSTINCTS, AND TRUST HIMSELF.

ONE THING HE'D ALWAYS DREAMED OF DOING, LIKE HIS HEROES GENE AUTRY, ELVIS, SINATRA - WAS TO BE AN ACTOR IN FILM.

AND ONE THING THAT COMES WITH MASSIVE SUCCESS IS OPPORTUNITY.

You're a natural, Willie. As a singer and musician, you're naturally relaxed. As an actor, I think that same quality would come through.

Thank you for saying that.

WILLIE THOUGHT THE BEST WAY TO WORK HIS WAY INTO REDFORD'S NEWEST MOVIE, THE ELECTRIC HORSEMAN, WAS TO CALL UP THE DIRECTOR SYDNEY POLLACK, AND ASK HIM DIRECTLY.

Put me in that movie you're making with Bob and Jane Fonda.

Ha! Come to think of it, you might be right for the part of Redford's Manager.

AND IT WORKED OUT QUITE WELL. THE MOVIE, AND WILLIE'S PERFORMANCE, RECEIVED FAVORABLE REVIEWS.

IT WAS SUCH A POSITIVE AND REWARDING NEW EXPERIENCE FOR WILLIE, THAT HE WAS EXCITED TO TAKE ON MORE ACTING WORK.

HIS NEXT FILM, HONEYSUCKLE ROSE, WAS PRODUCED BY SYDNEY POLLACK, WHERE HE PLAYED, AGAIN, A VERSION OF HIMSELF.

WHILE ON A PRIVATE PLANE TOGETHER WITH SYDNEY POLLACK AND DIRECTOR JERRY SCHATZBERG, THE IDEA OF A SONG FOR THE SOUNDTRACK CAME UP.

What do you think it should be about?

Being on the road?

THAT WAS ALL WILLIE NEEDED TO HEAR.

"On The Road Again"?

THAT'S IT!

BY THE TIME THE PLANE TOUCHED DOWN IN L.A., WILLIE HAD THE SONG, COMPLETE WITH MELODY.

On the road again
Just can't wait to get on the road again
The life I love is making music with my friends
And I can't wait to be on the road again
On the road again
Going places I ain't never been
Seeing things that I may never see again
And I can't wait to get on the road again

'ON THE ROAD AGAIN' EVENTUALLY BECAME A MASSIVE HIT, AND SECURED AN OSCAR NOMINATION FOR BEST ORIGINAL SONG.

THE FILM WORK KEPT COMING HIS WAY, AND WILLIE WAS FULLY ENJOYING THIS UNIQUE PERK OF MAINSTREAM SUCCESS.

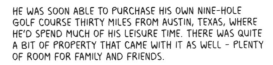

ANOTHER NOTABLE PERK IS BEING FREE TO DO THE THINGS ONE LOVES. ONE OF THOSE THINGS, FOR WILLIE, WAS GOLF.

HE WAS SOON ABLE TO PURCHASE HIS OWN NINE-HOLE GOLF COURSE THIRTY MILES FROM AUSTIN, TEXAS, WHERE HE'D SPEND MUCH OF HIS LEISURE TIME. THERE WAS QUITE A BIT OF PROPERTY THAT CAME WITH IT AS WELL - PLENTY OF ROOM FOR FAMILY AND FRIENDS.

PEDERNALES WAS THE PERFECT SETTING FOR WILLIE'S FOURTH OF JULY PICNIC - AND THE EVENT WAS HELD THERE IN 1979 AND 1980.

AS THE SEVENTIES DREW TO A CLOSE, WILLIE ALSO LOST TWO IMPORTANT PEOPLE IN HIS LIFE - HIS FATHER, IRA DOYLE NELSON, AND HIS GRANDMOTHER, MAMA NELSON.

THEY BOTH LIVED TO SEE HIS SUCCESS AND SUPPORT HIM THROUGHOUT HIS EARLY STRUGGLES.

THE PEDERNALES PROPERTY WAS LARGE ENOUGH TO FIT A BRAND NEW RECORDING STUDIO – AND IT QUICKLY BECAME A WHO'S WHO OF MUSICIANS COMING THROUGH.

SOON WILLIE HAD ENOUGH DUETS TO RELEASE A RECORD. HE TITLED THE RELEASE 'HALF NELSON.'

THROUGHOUT THE NEXT PHASE OF HIS CAREER, HE WOULD RUB ELBOWS WITH ALL KINDS OF HIGH STATUS CELEBRITIES AND MUSICIANS.

BUT WILLIE'S PERSONAL LIFE STILL HAD ITS SHARE OF DRAMA EVERY SO OFTEN.

IN 1983, CONNIE FOUND OUT WILLIE WAS HAVING AN AFFAIR WITH HIS 'HONEYSUCKLE ROSE' CO-STAR AMY IRVING, AND SHE FLEW TO PEDERNALES FROM COLORADO TO CONFRONT THEM BOTH.

WHEN WILLIE OPENED THE DOOR IN THE MIDDLE OF THE NIGHT, CONNIE BROKE HER HAND TRYING TO ATTACK HIM, WHILE ALSO SHOUTING FOR AMY TO COME DOWNSTAIRS.

77

IN DECEMBER 1983, WILLIE'S MOTHER MYRLE PASSED AWAY. LUNG CANCER WAS THE CULPRIT - THE SAME FATE OF HIS FATHER IRA.

SHE DIDN'T HAVE A TRADITIONAL RELATIONSHIP WITH WILLIE AND SISTER BOBBIE, BUT SHE LIVED HER LIFE IN HER OWN GYPSY-LIKE MANNER. SHE WAS A REBEL, AND SHE PASSED HER UNIQUE SPIRIT ONTO HER CHILDREN THE WAY THAT ONLY SHE COULD.

CONTINUING WILLIE'S FASCINATION WITH FILM, HE EVENTUALLY WAS ABLE TO BRING HIS LANDMARK 'RED HEADED STRANGER' ALBUM TO LIFE ON THE BIG SCREEN, IN 1985.

ORIGINALLY PITCHED AS A FILM STARRING ROBERT REDFORD, IT WAS ULTIMATELY WILLIE THAT ENDED UP ACTING IN THE TITLE ROLE. HE PARTLY FINANCED THE MOVIE HIMSELF AS WELL.

WILLIE SOLD THE FINISHED FILM TO PRODUCER SHEP GORDON, WHO ALSO HAPPENED TO BE ALICE COOPER'S LONGTIME MANAGER.

WILLIE EVEN GOT TO KEEP THE OLD WESTERN TOWN, BUILT FOR THE MOVIE ON THE PERIPHERY OF HIS PROPERTY - CALLED LUCK, TEXAS. IT BECAME A GREAT MEETING PLACE FOR EVENTS, PHOTOSHOOTS AND A GROWN-UP CLUBHOUSE FOR WILLIE AND VISITORS.

IN 1985, THE SPIRIT OF GIVING, HANDED DOWN FROM MAMA AND DADDY NELSON, INSPIRED WILLIE TO TRY AND COME TO THE RESCUE OF THE STRUGGLING AMERICAN FAMILY FARMER.

The American family farmer could use a hand, too.

BOB DYLAN MADE A COMMENT ABOUT THE SUBJECT DURING THE MASSIVE LIVE AID CONCERT, AND WILLIE BEGAN TO BRAINSTORM.

THE WHEELS STARTED TURNING FOR WILLIE. WHILE PASSING THROUGH ILLINOIS - PLAYING THE STATE FAIR, THE GOVERNOR JIM THOMPSON VISITED WILLIE'S BUS.

The farmers are having a rough year, Willie. There's a federal farm bill coming up, but there's lots of issues.

WILLIE DECIDED TO PUT TOGETHER A BENEFIT CONCERT - IT WOULD BE CALLED, SIMPLY ENOUGH, FARM AID.

HE CALLED HIS FRIENDS BOB DYLAN, NEIL YOUNG, AND JOHN MELLENCAMP TO PERFORM.

IT ALL CAME TOGETHER FOR WILLIE AND THE ORGANIZERS. 80,000 PEOPLE SHOWED UP AT UNIVERSITY OF ILLINOIS' MEMORIAL STADIUM TO HEAR SOME OF THE 20TH CENTURY'S BIGGEST ACTS.

BILLY JOEL, B.B. KING, ROY ORBISON, JOHNNY CASH, CHARLEY PRIDE, AND MORE ALL DAZZLED THE CROWD.

THAT FIRST FARM AID CONCERT RAISED 7 MILLION DOLLARS FOR FAMILY FARMERS ACROSS AMERICA.

THE MORE WILLIE RESEARCHED THE TOPIC, THE MORE HE WANTED TO GET INVOLVED AND HELP HOWEVER HE COULD.

HE EVEN WENT TO WASHINGTON, D.C. TO TESTIFY BEFORE A SENATE COMMITTEE ABOUT THE RECENT STRUGGLES AND DWINDLING NUMBERS OF U.S. FAMILY FARMERS.

WILLIE AND THE REST OF THE ORGANIZERS DECIDED FARM AID SHOULD BE AN ANNUAL EVENT. THE CONCERT AND ORGANIZATION HAS CONTINUED TO PROVIDE ASSISTANCE TO FAMILY FARMERS FOR OVER 30 YEARS.

BY THE SECOND HALF OF THE EIGHTIES, WILLIE HAD BEEN SO PROLIFIC, CAPITALIZING ON THE SUCCESS OF HIS RECORDS, THAT HE'D FLOODED THE MARKET WITH MORE RELEASES.

SALES BEGAN TO TAKE A DIVE OVERALL.

COUNTRY MUSIC HAD CHANGED SINCE THE OUTLAW DAYS – AND WILLIE BECAME AN ELDER STATESMAN. JOHNNY CASH, WAYLON JENNINGS, KRIS KRISTOFFERSON HAD ALSO SEEN BETTER DAYS IN TERMS OF SALES AND POPULARITY.

THE IDEA TO FORM A SORT OF SUPERGROUP STARTED FROM A CONVERSATION WITH JOHNNY CASH.

You know, you've made a record with everybody in the world except me.

We should do one together.

JOHNNY CASH WAS PUTTING TOGETHER A CHRISTMAS CONCERT IN SWITZERLAND, IN 1984, AND SUGGESTED THEY GO INTO THE STUDIO IN NASHVILLE BEFOREHAND.

WHEN WAYLON, WILLIE, KRIS AND JOHNNY GOT TOGETHER, THEY RECORDED A SONG CALLED 'THE HIGHWAYMAN' WRITTEN BY JIMMY WEBB.

THE PRODUCER CHIPS MOMAN WAS ALSO ON BOARD, AND THE REST OF THE GROUP ALL BROUGHT SONGS TO THE TABLE – ENOUGH FOR A FULL ALBUM.

AND AT THAT CHRISTMAS CONCERT IN MONTREUX, SWITZERLAND, THE HIGHWAYMEN PERFORMED TOGETHER IN PUBLIC FOR THE FIRST TIME.

BY THE TIME WILLIE ARRIVED ON SET OF 'STAGECOACH,' HIS MARRIAGE TO CONNIE HAD FALLEN APART.

SHE PUT FINALLY PUT HER FOOT DOWN, AFTER YEARS OF WILLIE'S INFIDELITY. SHE DUMPED HIS BELONGINGS INTO A CABIN ON HIS PEDERNALES PROPERTY, AND SHE MOVED TO DEL MAR.

'STAGECOACH,' A MADE-FOR-TV MOVIE, WAS THE SECOND COLLABORATION BETWEEN THE MEMBERS OF THE HIGHWAYMEN.

THE MOVIE SET IN TUSCON WAS ALSO WHERE WILLIE MET ANN MARIE D'ANGELO - THE MAKEUP ARTIST ON THE MOVIE. EVERYONE CALLED HER ANNIE.

NATURALLY, EVERYONE ON A MOVIE SET GRAVITATES TOWARD CERTAIN PEOPLE - TO SHARE, OR HAVE A LAUGH. ANNIE AND WILLIE WERE THAT PERSON FOR ONE ANOTHER.

ANNIE WAS A FAN BEFORE SHE MET HIM, BUT SHE DIDN'T SEEM INTIMIDATED - SHE SAW WILLIE FOR WHO HE WAS. WILLIE FELT THAT AS WELL. HE ALSO LOVED THAT SHE SEEMED TO SPEAK HER MIND.

EVEN THOUGH ANNIE HAD MADE CLEAR, AS FAR AS DATING WAS CONCERNED, THAT SHE WOULDN'T GO NEAR CELEBRITIES, DIVORCED MEN OR SOMEONE WITH KIDS...SHE COULD SEE IN WILLIE THAT HE WAS SINCERE IN HIS INTENTIONS.

AS THE NINETIES CAME TO BE, WILLIE SEEMED TO BE RIDING HIGH ON A WAVE OF MAINSTREAM SUCCESS AND ACCEPTANCE. HE WAS ICONIC IN HIS PIGTAILS AND RED BANDANA - AND DEFINITELY A HOUSEHOLD NAME.

WILLIE WAS SO RECOGNIZABLE BY THIS POINT, HE SIGNED ON TO DO MANY CORPORATE ENDORSEMENTS - LONE STAR BEER, NEW BALANCE SHOES, JOSE CUERVO TEQUILA, WRANGLER JEANS AND MORE.

IN APRIL 1990, FARM AID IV WAS HELD IN INDIANAPOLIS. GUNS N' ROSES, ELTON JOHN, LOU REED, BONNIE RAITT AND MORE PLAYED TO A CROWD OF 45,000. THE SHOW RAISED ANOTHER $1.2 MILLION FOR AMERICA'S STRUGGLING FAMILY FARMERS.

WILLIE HAD EVERYTHING HE COULD EVER WANT - RECOGNITION, SUCCESS, LOVE, AND FAMILY. IT SEEMED THAT FOR A TIME, NOTHING COULD GO WRONG.

BUT SOON, HE LOST EVERYTHING.

CHAPTER 7

★ ELDER STATESMAN ★

IN THE FALL OF 1991, WILLIE AND ANNIE WERE MARRIED, AS THEIR TWO YOUNG SONS, LUKAS AUTRY AND JACOB MICAH LOOKED ON.

FOR A BRIEF PERIOD THEREAFTER, THE NELSON FAMILY WERE DETERMINED TO LIVE A HUMBLE LIFE IN THE OLD HOMETOWN OF ABBOTT, TEXAS. WILLIE HAD PURCHASED THE HOME OF A FAMILY FRIEND.

WORD GOT AROUND QUITE FAST, AS YOU'D EXPECT IN SUCH A SMALL TOWN, AND WILLIE REALIZED HE'D PUT HIS FAMILY IN A VULNERABLE SITUATION. ANYONE COULD WALK UP TO THEIR HOUSE – AND MANY TIMES THEY WOULD.

HI WILLIE!

THE DECISION WAS MADE TO CHANGE THEIR MAIN RESIDENCE TO HAWAII, A MORE PRIVATE AND SECLUDED LIFE FOR THEIR CHILDREN– BUT ALSO RICH WITH BEAUTY AND CULTURE.

THEY WOULD KEEP THEIR HOMES IN ABOTT AND IN TENNESSEE AS WELL, SINCE THEY COULD AFFORD TO AT THAT POINT.

WILLIE NELSON JR. WAS ONLY ONE OF THE FAMILY MEMBERS STILL LIVING IN ONE OF THE RIDGETOP, TENNESSEE PROPERTIES. BEING WILLIE'S OLDEST SON, HE HAD A COMPLICATED LIFE.

BILLY WAS A TALENTED MUSICIAN IN HIS OWN RIGHT, BUT HAD SOMEWHAT OF A WILD STREAK, HENCE HIS NICKNAME 'WILD BILL.'

IN DECEMBER 1991, AT 33 YEARS OLD, HE PASSED AWAY TRAGICALLY BY SUICIDE.

MY BODY'S JUST A SUITCASE FOR MY SOOOUUULL...

IN THE IMMEDIATE AFTERMATH OF HIS SON'S PASSING, WILLIE AND HIS FAMILY CHOSE TO RETREAT TO HAWAII.

USED TO BEING ON THE ROAD HIS WHOLE LIFE, STAYING PUT WASN'T HELPING MUCH IN HIS GRIEVING.

HE PLAYED A NEW YEARS EVE SHOW IN BRANSON, MISSOURI, ONLY A FEW DAYS LATER. DESPITE THE CIRCUMSTANCES, WILLIE STILL STAYED LONG AFTERWARDS, AS HE OFTEN DOES, TO SIGN EVERY AUTOGRAPH HE COULD.

TO MAKE MATTERS WORSE, EARLIER THAT YEAR, A DOZEN IRS AGENTS SWARMED ONTO WILLIE'S PEDERNALES GOLF COURSE TO ARREST HIM.

IT SEEMED HIS FINANCES WERE SO MISMANAGED TO THE POINT WHERE HE OWED THE GOVERNMENT MILLIONS OF DOLLARS IN BACK TAXES.

NOT ONLY DID THEY ARREST WILLIE, BUT THEY SEIZED PROPERTY IN SEVERAL OF HIS HOMES, AND PADLOCKED HIS RECORDING STUDIO.

THE FEDS WERE CONVINCED WILLIE WAS HOARDING MONEY SOMEWHERE.

THIS QUICKLY BECAME A VERY PUBLIC PROBLEM FOR WILLIE, AND IT WOUDN'T BE RESOLVED WITHOUT A FIGHT.

NEIL RESHEN, WILLIE'S OUTSPOKEN FORMER MANAGER, HAD PREVIOUSLY CLAIMED HE WAS A "TAX EXPERT", AND HAD "ONE OF THE BEST TAX MINDS OF ANYONE IN THE COUNTRY."

THIS PROVED TO BE UNTRUE AFTER THE IRS DISALLOWED THE TAX SHELTERS AND LOOPHOLES HE'D BEEN USING OVER THE YEARS.

THERE WAS PRESSURE FOR WILLIE TO GIVE UP, IN A SENSE, AND DECLARE BANKRUPTCY. WILLIE, ENCOURAGED BY HIS MANAGER MARK ROTHBAUM, ULTIMATELY CHOSE TO FIGHT THE PROBLEM CREATIVELY, AND AGGRESSIVELY.

AFTER NEGOTIATIONS WITH THE IRS, BOTH PARTIES DECIDED ON A UNIQUE SOLUTION. USING THE MASTER TAPES THAT THE GOVERNMENT HAD SEIZED, WILLIE AND THE IRS PARTNERED IN RELEASING A UNIQUE DOUBLE ALBUM, WITH THE PROFITS GOING TOWARDS HIS DEBT.

THE ALBUM WAS CALLED 'THE IRS TAPES: WHO'LL BUY MY MEMORIES?' AND IT WAS ADVERTISED DIRECTLY TO FANS THROUGH A TELEVISION ADVERTISEMENT.

THAT ALBUM, AND A FOLLOW-UP RELEASE CALLED 'THE HUNGRY YEARS' DIDN'T SELL QUITE ENOUGH TO PAY OFF THE TAX BILL, BUT THE IRS SOON DROPPED THE CASE AFTER WILLIE PAID A REDUCED AMOUNT OF 6 MILLION DOLLARS.

THOUGH SEEMINGLY DEVASTATED BY RECENT EVENTS, WILLIE STILL MANAGES TO STAY AND THINK POSITIVELY THROUGHOUT.

AFTER THE INITIAL VERY ROUGH ROAD INTO THE 1990'S, WILLIE ENJOYED HIS GROWING ELDER STATESMAN STATUS IN COUNTRY MUSIC AND OVERALL MAINSTREAM OF POP CULTURE.

COUNTRY MUSIC HALL OF FAME INDUCTION, 1993.

HIS SPORADIC APPEARANCES IN MOVIES CONTINUED AS WELL.

WILLIE AND FAMILY CONTINUED, AS THEY OFTEN DID, TO PERFORM AS MUCH AS THEY COULD.

IN 1994, WILLIE WAS DRIVING BY HIMSELF BACK FROM ABBOTT TO WACO, TEXAS. HE'D PULLED OVER TO GET SOME SLEEP IN THE BACKSEAT, WHEN HE WAS STARTLED AWAKE BY A POLICE OFFICER BANGING ON THE WINDOW.

TAP TAP—

HE HAPPENED TO HAVE A JOINT IN THE CAR'S ASHTRAY, AND A LITTLE MORE UNDER THE PASSENGER SEAT. HE WAS ARRESTED, BUT THE CASE WAS DROPPED.

THE OFFICERS HAD TURNED OFF THEIR RECORDING WHILE DOING THE SEARCH, AND COULDN'T GIVE A REASON WHY.

HE CAME BACK TO WACO TO PLAY MUSIC FOR THE SHERIFF'S ASSOCIATION OF TEXAS, AS A SHOW OF GOOD FAITH TOWARDS THE POLICE THERE. AFTER ALL, IT WASN'T THEM HE WAS AGAINST. IT WAS THE MARIJUANA LAWS HE FELT WERE UNJUST.

IT'D BE BETTER FOR EVERYONE IF WE LEGALIZED MARIJUANA, REGULATED IT AND TAXED IT LIKE WE TAX CIGARETTES.

ONLY A FEW PEOPLE CLAPPED.

THROUGHOUT THE DECADE, WILLIE EXPERIMENTED WITH MANY STYLES AND GENRES, AS HAS BEEN THE CASE HIS WHOLE LIFE. HE ALSO ENJOYED COLLABORATING WITH OLD AND NEW FRIENDS, LIKE BOB DYLAN, PAUL SIMON AND SNOOP DOGG.

HE MADE BIG, HIGH PROFILE, PRODUCTION HEAVY RECORDS LIKE 'THE GREAT DIVIDE' - PRODUCED BY MATT SERLETIC, WHO WAS FRESH OFF A HUGE SUCCESS PRODUCING SANTANA'S 'SUPERNATURAL' COMEBACK CROSSOVER ALBUM.

BUT WILLIE ALSO WENT INWARD AND CHOSE TO RECORD AN ALBUM LIKE 'SPIRIT' - AS BARE BONES AS A RECORD COULD BE - IN THE SAME VEIN AS RED HEADED STRANGER, BUT EVEN MORE MINIMAL AND SPARE.

ANOTHER NOTABLE ALBUM WAS THE DANIEL LANOIS-PRODUCED 'TEATRO,' WHICH FEATURED MANY OF HIS VERY EARLIEST SONGS RE-RECORDED. THEY RECORDED, WITH HAUNTING BACKING VOCALS BY EMMYLOU HARRIS - IN AN OLD ABANDONED MOVIE THEATER.

THE OLD SONGS, LIKE 'HOME MOTEL,' WERE GIVEN NEW LIFE AND A TIMELESS, MELANCHOLY SENSIBILITY.

WILLIE AND FAMILY PLAYED A SOLID SET OF SONGS AT THE HISTORIC BUT DISASTROUS WOODSTOCK '99 FESTIVAL.

SHORTLY AFTER THE NEW CENTURY BEGAN, WILLIE BEGAN LOSING MANY GOOD FRIENDS AND PEERS, LIKE WAYLON JENNINGS AND JOHNNY CASH.

WELL INTO THE 2000'S, WILLIE CONTINUED TO RELEASE ALBUMS AND TOUR AT A RAPID PACE. PART OF THE REASON HE'S SO PROLIFIC IS HIS FRIEND, PRODUCER AND CO-WRITER BUDDY CANNON.

HE HAS BECOME WILLIE'S MOST CONSISTENT WRITING PARTNER, SOMETIMES TEXT MESSAGING SONG LYRICS BACK TO EACH OTHER WHEN THEY AREN'T ABLE TO COLLABORATE IN PERSON.

WILLIE HAS NEVER CEASED HIS ACTIVISM WHEN IT COMES TO MARIJUANA. HE PREFERS VAPORIZING THE CANNABIS THESE DAYS DUE TO AGING LUNGS, BUT WANTS TO SEE ALL FORMS OF THE MEDICINE LEGALIZED FOR ITS BENEFICIAL EFFECTS.

HE'S SPOKEN OF THE POTENTIAL USES FOR THE HEMP PLANT, WHICH IS CANNABIS AS WELL - JUST WITHOUT MOST OF THE THC PRESENT. IT CAN BE USED FOR AGRICULTURE, CLOTHING, PAIN RELIEF, AND MORE. THIS IS THE SOURCE FOR THE CURRENT CBD CRAZE.

WILLIE, ALONG WITH HIS WIFE ANNIE AND OTHERS, STARTED THEIR OWN CANNABIS VENTURE CALLED 'WILLIE'S RESERVE,' SOURCING ITS PRODUCTS FROM SMALL FARMS ACROSS THE USA - JUST AS POT'S LEGAL STATUS WAS STARTING TO BECOME A REALITY. A CBD COMPANY CALLED 'WILLIE'S REMEDY' WAS LAUNCHED A FEW YEARS AFTER.

WHAT'S THIS ONE CALLED AGAIN?

WILLIE, NOW WELL INTO HIS EIGHTIES, IS ENJOYING ANOTHER PROLIFIC PERIOD. WITH BUDDY CANNON'S HELP, WILLIE'S RECENT ALBUMS, LIKE 'BAND OF BROTHERS,' 'GOD'S PROBLEM CHILD' AND OTHERS, HAVE REACHED THE TOP OF THE ALBUM CHARTS UPON THEIR RELEASE.

REGARDLESS OF THE SUCCESS OF ANY ONE ALBUM, WILLIE HAS CONTINUED TO TOUR RELENTLESSLY. HE'S A RESTLESS SPIRIT AND ENJOYS LIFE **ON THE ROAD - AGAIN AND AGAIN.**

HE CONTINUES TO PERFORM AND RECORD AT A PACE MANY WOULD DEEM GRUELING.

FOR WILLIE, IT'S SIMPLY WHAT HE DOES, AND WHAT HE'S ALWAYS DONE.

FOR A HUMBLE PICKER FROM ABBOTT, SUCCESS ISN'T MEASURED BY ALBUMS OR TICKETS SOLD.

SUCCESS IS DETERMINED BY LIVING THE LIFE YOU WANT, SURROUNDED BY PEOPLE YOU LOVE.

TO THIS DAY, WHEN WILLIE GETS IN A CAR AND DRIVES DOWN ANY LONELY HIGHWAY...

THE MUSIC, STILL, FLOWS FREELY.

AND THE SONGS, STILL, SEEM TO COME OUT OF THIN AIR.

THE END.

★ BIBLIOGRAPHY ★

Nelson, Willie, with David Ritz. (2015). *It's a Long Story: My Life*. New York, NY: Little, Brown and Company.

Patoski, Joe Nick. (2008). *Willie Nelson: An Epic Life*. New York, NY: Little, Brown and Company.

Nelson, Susie. (1987). *Heartworn Memories: A Daughter's personal biography of Willie Nelson*. Austin, Texas: Eakin Publications, Inc.

Nelson, Willie. (2012) *Roll Me Up and Smoke Me When I Die: Musings From The Road*. New York, NY: William Morrow, An Imprint Of HarperCollins Publishers.

Doyle, Patrick. (2019, April). The High Life. Rolling Stone, Issue 1327.

★ SONG CREDITS ★

"New San Antonio Rose"
Written by Bob Wills
© EMI Blackwood Music Inc., Sony/ATV Songs LLC, Jesse Belle Denver, Bourne Co., Chrysalis One Songs LLC, BOURNE CO, BMG Rights Management (Ireland) Ltd

"Family Bible"
Written by Walter M. Breeland, Paul F. Buskirk, and Claude Gray.
© Glad Music Publishing & Recording LP and Pappy Daily Music LP.

"Night Life"
Written by Walter Breeland, Paul F. Buskirk & Willie Nelson
© 1962 Sony/ATV Tree Publishing, Glad Music Publishing & Recording LP, Pappy Daily Music LP.

"Crazy"
Written by Willie Nelson
© 1961 Sony/ATV Tree Publishing

"On The Road Again"
Written by Willie Nelson
© 1980 Full Nelson Music Inc.

"My Body's Just a Suitcase for My Soul"
Written by Mae Axton, Ed Honeycut and Roger Alan Wade
© 2015 Promised Land Music

"Healing Hands Of Time"
Written By Willie Nelson
© 1965 Sony/ATV Tree Publishing

"Red Headed Stranger"
Written by Edith Lindeman and Carl Stutz
© 1954 Lindeman/Stutz

"Seven Spanish Angels"
Written by Eddie F. Setser and Troy Harold Seals
© 1982 Warner Chappell Music, Inc

Also available from NBM Comics Biographies:

THE BEATLES IN COMICS!
Various authors, Michels Mabel

THE TRUE DEATH OF BILLY THE KID
Rick Geary

The Provocative COLETTE
Annie Goetzinger & Rodolphe

Philip K. DICK
A Comics Biography
Laurent Queyssi, writer, Mauro Marchesi, art

Albert EINSTEIN, The Poetry of Real
Manuel Garcia Iglesias, Marwan Kahil

ELVIS
Philippe Chanoinat and Fabrice Le Henanff

GHETTO BROTHER- Warrior to Peacemaker
Julian Voloj, Claudia Ahlering

GIRL IN DIOR
Annie Goetzinger

GLENN GOULD: A Life Off Tempo
Sandrine Revel

BILLIE HOLIDAY
José Muñoz, Carlos Sampayo

LEONARDO DA VINCI
Marwan Kahil, Ariel Vittori

MARIE ANTOINETTE, PHANTOM QUEEN
Annie Goetzinger & Rodolphe

BOB MARLEY IN COMICS
Gaet's, Sophie Blitman

MONET: Itinerant of Light
Efa, Salva Rubio

NIKI DE SAINT PHALLE
The Garden of Secrets
Dominique Osuch, Sandrine Martin

RODIN
Eddy Simon, Joel Alessandra

The ROLLING STONES in Comics!
Ceka and various artists

SARTRE
Mathilde Ramadier & Anais Depommier

TAMBA, Child Soldier
Marion Achard, writer; Yan Degruel, art

THOREAU, A Sublime Life
A. Dan, Maximilien Le Roy

We have hundreds of graphic novels
See more at:
NBMPUB.COM

NBM
160 Broadway, Suite 700, East Wing
New York, NY 10038
Catalog upon request

THE BEATLES
in comics
nbm

Elvis
nbm

LEONARDO DA VINCI
nbm

A. Rodin
MUSÉE RODIN PARIS
nbm

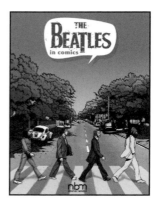

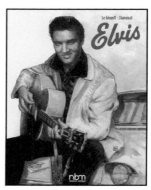

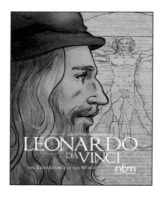

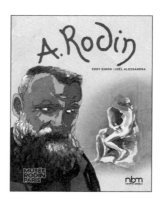

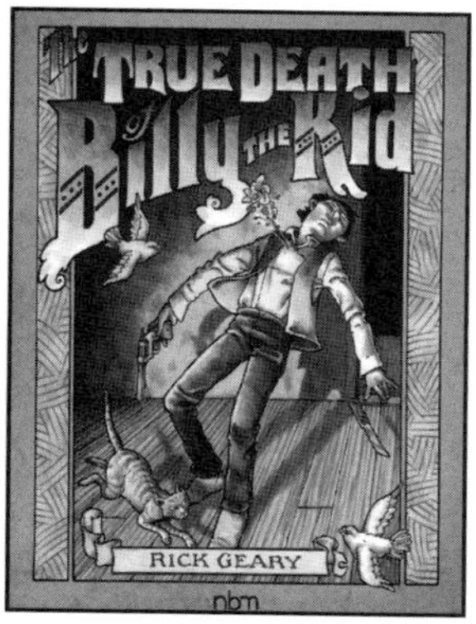
The True Death of Billy the Kid
Rick Geary

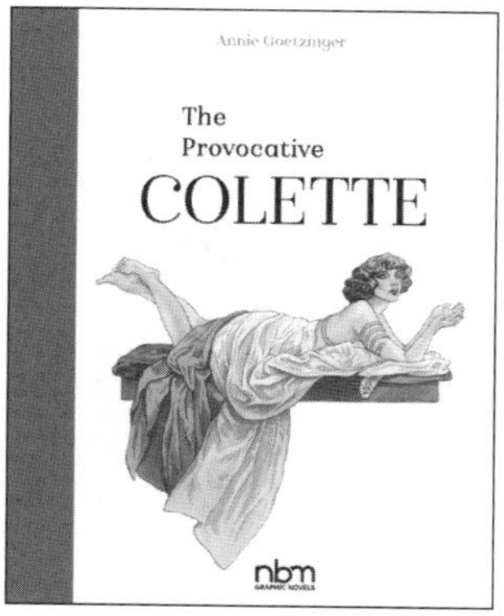
Annie Goetzinger
The Provocative
COLETTE

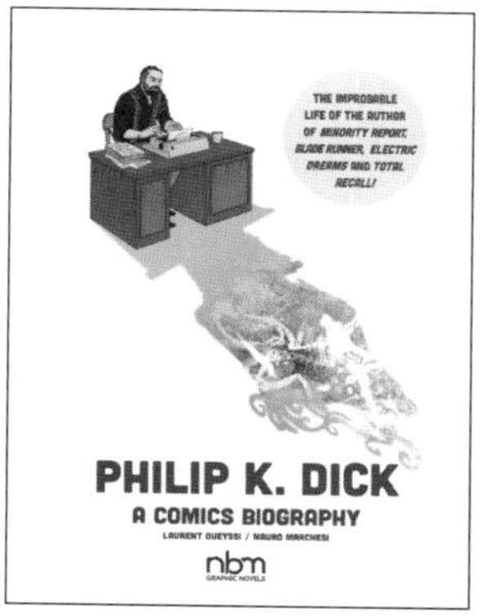
THE IMPROBABLE LIFE OF THE AUTHOR OF MINORITY REPORT, BLADE RUNNER, ELECTRIC DREAMS AND TOTAL RECALL!
PHILIP K. DICK
A COMICS BIOGRAPHY
LAURENT QUEYSSI / MAURO MARCHESI

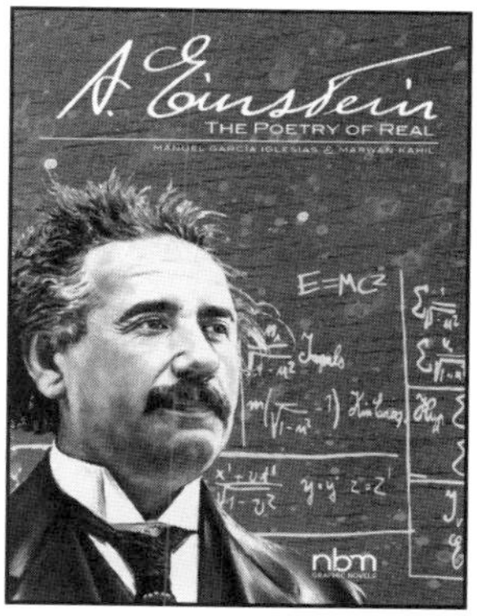
A. Einstein
THE POETRY OF REAL
MANUEL GARCÍA IGLESIAS & MARWAN KAHIL
E=MC²

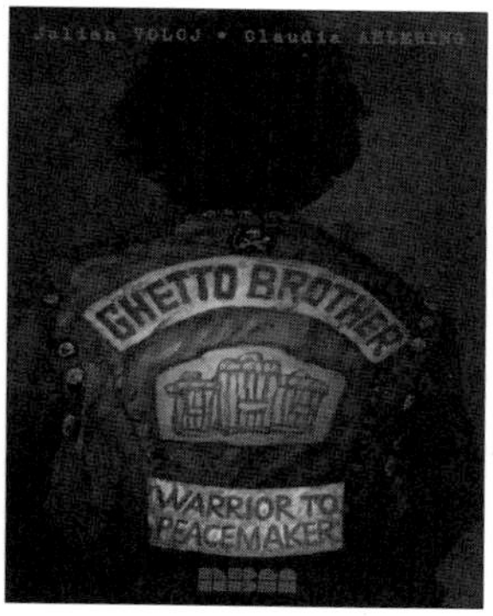
Julian VOLOJ • Claudia AHLERING
GHETTO BROTHER
WARRIOR TO PEACEMAKER

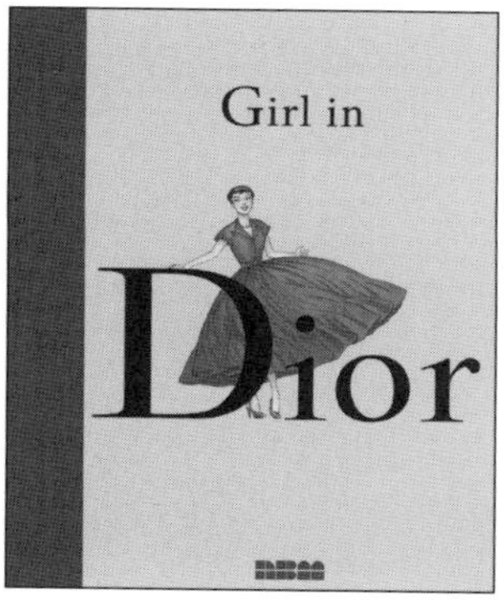
Girl in
Dior

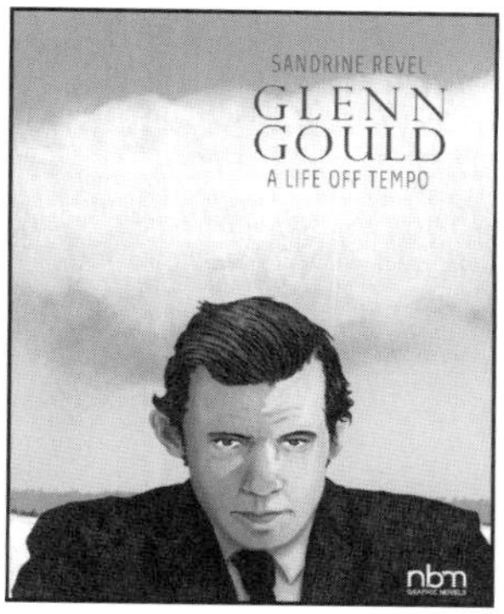
SANDRINE REVEL
GLENN GOULD
A LIFE OFF TEMPO

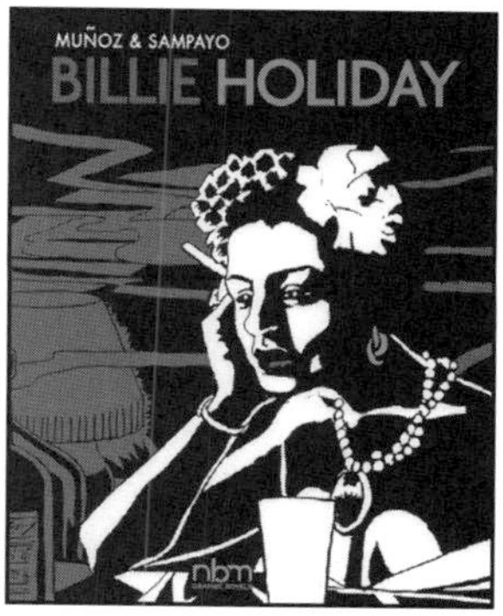
MUÑOZ & SAMPAYO
BILLIE HOLIDAY

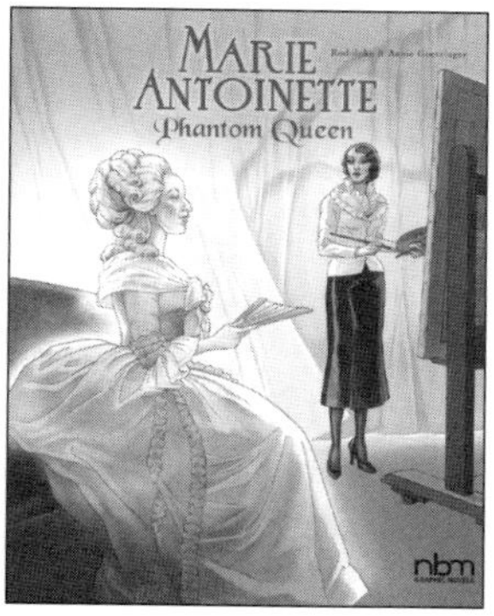
MARIE ANTOINETTE
Phantom Queen

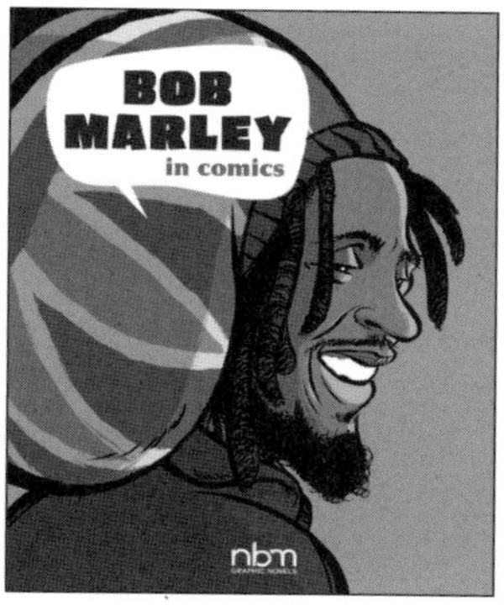
BOB MARLEY
in comics

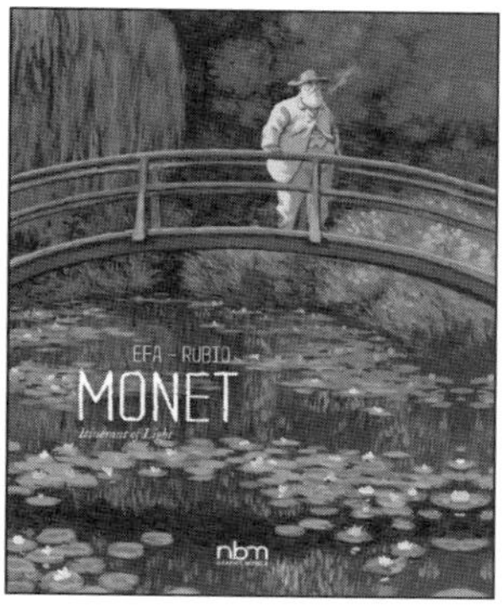
EFA - RUBIO
MONET

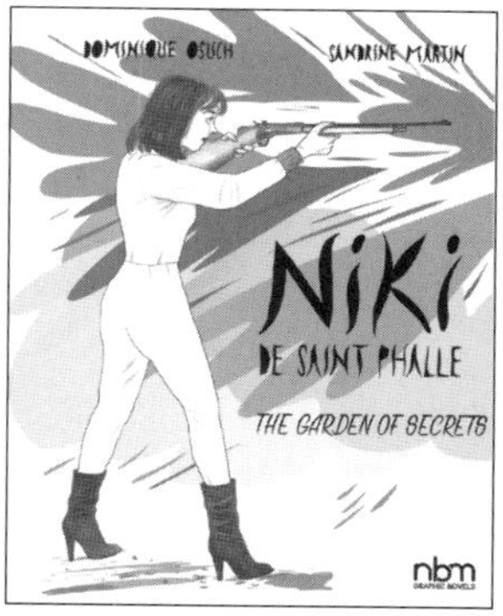
DOMINIQUE OSUCH
SANDRINE MARTIN
NIKI
DE SAINT PHALLE
THE GARDEN OF SECRETS

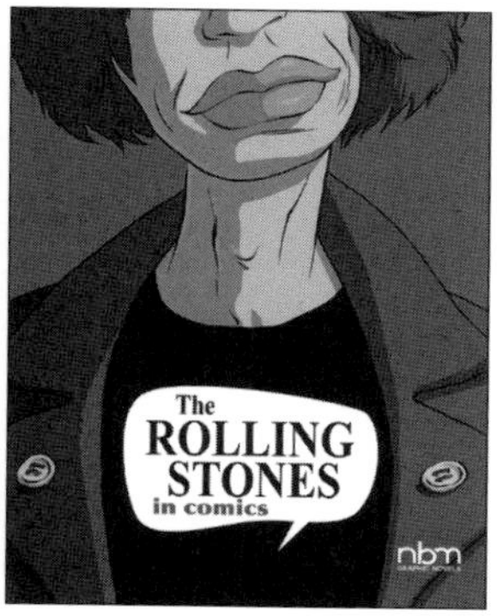
The ROLLING STONES
in comics

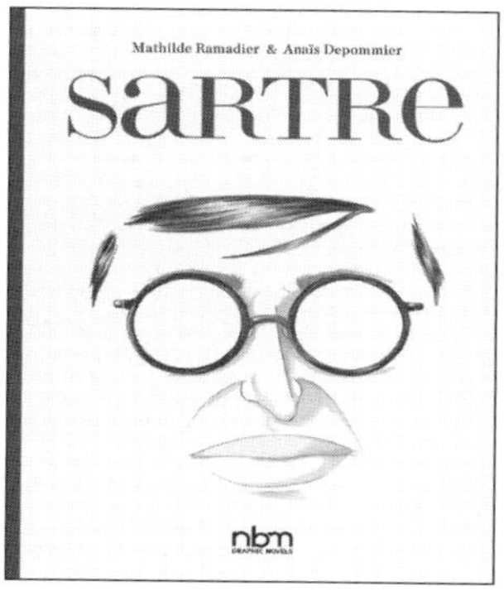
Mathilde Ramadier & Anaïs Depommier
SARTRE

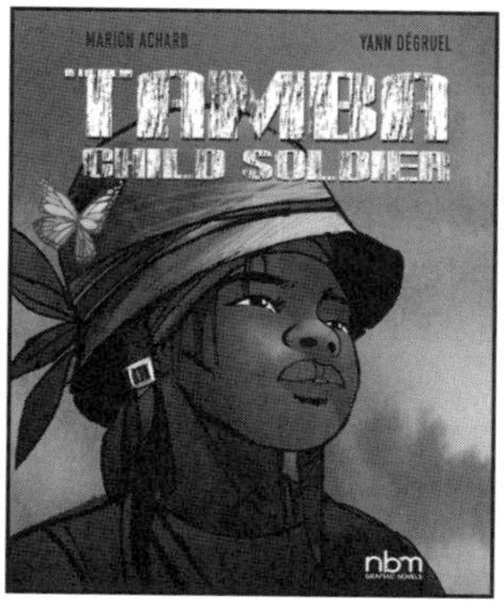
MARION ACHARD
YANN DÉGRUEL
TAMBA
CHILD SOLDIER

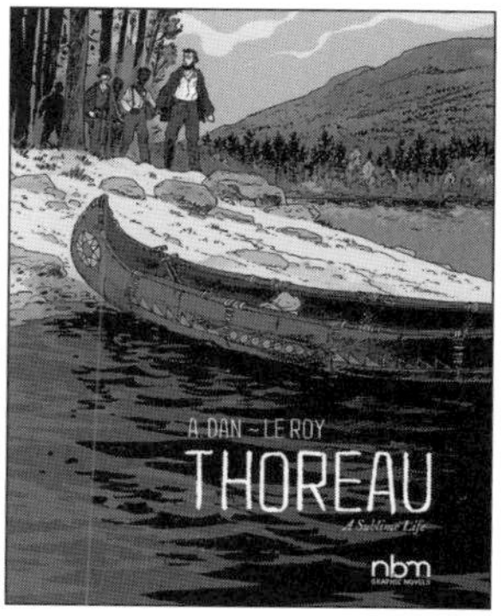
A. DAN ~ LE ROY
THOREAU
A Sublime Life

Other graphic novels from NBM:

RED MOTHER WITH CHILD
Christian Lax

PHOOLAN DEVI, Rebel Queen
Claire Fauvel

GIANT
Mikael

See more at **NBMPUB.COM**

Christian Lax
RED MOTHER WITH CHILD
nbm

Claire Fauvel
PHOOLAN DEVI
REBEL QUEEN
nbm

MIKAEL
GIANT
nbm

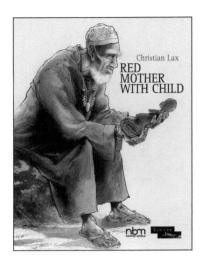

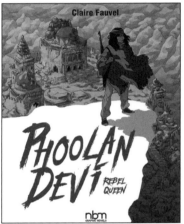

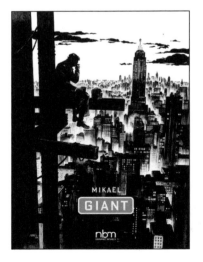

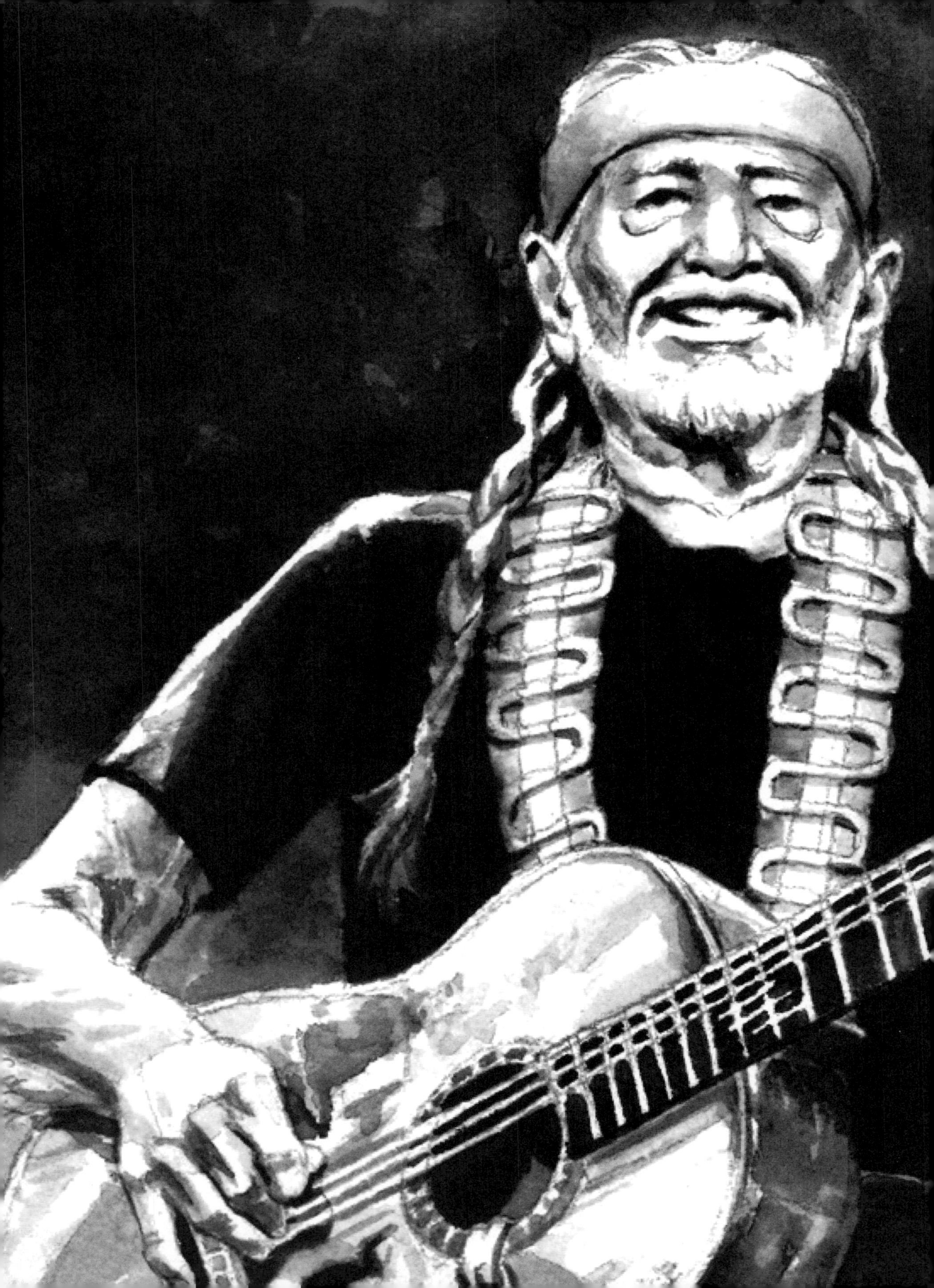